# Tyrants and Conquerors

# TYRANTS AND CONQUERORS

*Fon W. Boardman, Jr.*

HENRY Z. WALCK, INC.

A Division of David McKay Company, Inc.

New York

920

Library of Congress Cataloging in Publication Data

Boardman, Fon Wyman, 1911-
    Tyrants and conquerors.

    SUMMARY: Includes biographies of such notorious
tyrants as Nero, Tamerlane, Attila, and Hitler and
discusses the characteristics that constitute a tyrant or a conqueror.
    1. Dictators—Biography—Juvenile literature.
2. Biography—Juvenile literature. [1. Dictators]
I. Onyshkewych, Zenkowij.  II.  Title.
D107.B6     909'.2'2 [B]   [920]     77-10899
ISBN 0-8098-0010-1

10  9  8  7  6  5  4  3  2  1
Manufactured in the United States of America

# Contents

Who Is a Tyrant? What Is a Conqueror?   1

Shih Huang-ti: Unity Through Bloodshed   7

Nero: The Tyrant as Coward   27

Attila: Conqueror Without Roots   47

Jenghiz Khan: Conquest for Conquest's Sake   67

Tamerlane: Bloodshed for the Sake of Bloodshed   87

Muhammad II: Conquest for Religion's Sake   103

Ivan the Terrible: The Tyrant as Madman   123

Adolf Hitler: The Tyrant as Living Evil   143

Are "Great Men" Great?   169

For Further Reading   173

Index   177

C.1

# Tyrants and Conquerors

# Who Is a Tyrant?

# What Is a Conqueror?

A tyrant, says the *Oxford English Dictionary*, is "an absolute ruler." Strictly speaking, a tyrant as a ruler can be good, bad or indifferent. But the dictionary also says that *tyrant* can mean "a king or ruler who exercises his power in an oppressive, unjust, or cruel manner; a despot." This is the kind of image that usually comes to mind when we hear the word *tyrant*. The eight men discussed in this book all fit this definition very well.

Robert Herrick, the seventeenth century English poet, wrote that "kings seek their subjects' good; tyrants their own." This in effect defines all kings as good and takes that title away from any tyrannical ruler.

John Locke, the leading eighteenth century English philosopher, wrote that "wherever Law ends, Tyranny begins." In other words, a tyrant puts himself above the law, but when laws takes precedence over rulers, tyranny cannot flourish.

The French novelist Stendhal, who served in the army of a conqueror and tyrant, Napoleon Bonaparte, at the beginning of the nineteenth century, wrote:

> A tyrant may be intelligent or stupid, good or evil; whatever the case, he is both all-powerful, he is frightened by conspiracies, he is flattered, he is deceived; the prisons fill, the cowardly hypocrites whisper, and the silence becomes so complete that the heart almost stops.

This statement can be applied to each of the eight men whose lives are described in this book.

Taking a cynical view of human nature, Daniel Defoe (1660?–1731), another English author, thought "all men would be tyrants if they could."

Would someone forced to live under a tyrant rather be that tyrant? Perhaps this is what the American humorist and satirist Don Marquis (1878–1937) had in mind when he wrote: "If you are a tyrant you can arrange things so that most of the trouble happens to other people." The men in this book caused a great deal of trouble for a great many people.

As for conquerors, the *Oxford English Dictionary* simply says that a conqueror is "one who gains possession of a country, etc., by force of arms; one who subdues or subjugates a nation." Being a factual dictionary definition, this statement does not go into the legal or moral aspects of a conqueror's actions. A conqueror, of course, always finds grounds for justifying in his own mind his conquest of some other land and people, even though the people who suffer the conquest may see the matter in quite a different light.

The eight men in this book all lived, conquered and ruled in Asia or Europe, or both. While they are by no means the only major tyrants and conquerors in the history of the world, all of the others' careers also took place on those two continents. Except for the special case of the Spanish *conquistadores,* who conquered Latin America but had little to do with ruling it, the other continents—North America and Australia—were afflicted only with small-time tyrants. The Indians of North and South America were completely overcome, but not by any one conqueror. Latin America has abounded with minor tyrants such as François "Papa Doc" Duvalier, whose rule of Haiti from 1957 until his death in 1971 matched anything Ivan the Terrible did in brutality if not in quantity.

Were not George Washington (1732–99) and Simón Bolívar (1783–1830) conquerors? Not in the sense of taking a foreign land by force of arms. They were successful generals, the one in North America, the other in South America, but they fought in their own lands against a foreign government that ruled over them. To those on their side, they were not conquerors but liberators. In the eyes of those they fought against, they were traitors and revolutionaries.

The most active area for twentieth century tyrants, if not conquerors, is Africa, with its young and not-yet-stabilized nations that emerged from the rather sudden end of colonialism. Reporting on the leaders of three of these countries, the *New York Times* on February 27, 1977, said: "In private conversations with Africans, they are compared with Hitler, Stalin, the late 'Papa Doc' Duvalier of Haiti and Ivan the Terrible, and their sanity is questioned." The three men discussed were President Idi Amin of Uganda, some of whose actions are irrational and who, the *New Republic* declared, "is the latest in the twentieth century's unparalleled line of sovereign butchers—less terrifying than his predecessors only because, fortunately, he commands a small and impotent nation"; Jean Bedel Bokassa, who has taken what to outsiders must seem the preposterous step of proclaiming himself "emperor" of the Central African Republic and changing its name accordingly; and President Macias Ngueno of Equatorial Africa, who has ordered ears and hands to be cut off those guilty of petty thefts.

No women tyrants or conquerors have been named. Perhaps Catherine the Great (1729–96) of Russia qualifies. She had complete power, but she used it to effect some reforms and she thought of herself as an "enlightened despot." She became more conservative and more of a tyrant as her reign went on. Tz'u Hsi (1834–1908), regent and dowager empress of China, tried very hard to achieve tyrannical rule. Some might nominate Indira Gandhi, prime minister of India from 1966 to 1977, because of the way she suspended her country's constitution and ruled arbitrarily for a year and a half. To those opposed to tyranny, it was encouraging that the people of India, the moment they had a chance to vote, soundly rejected Mrs. Gandhi's rule by decree. There have been a few women military leaders in history, such as Boudicca (d. A.D.

61) in Roman Britain and Joan of Arc (1412–31) in France, but their careers ended in defeat, not conquest.

Granted that the eight men in this book were all famous and historically important tyrants or conquerers, why choose them instead of others? Cyrus the Great, Alexander the Great, Charlemagne, Napoleon Bonaparte and Joseph Stalin match any of the eight in both good and bad achievements and in importance. In addition, there are lesser tyrants and conquerors such as the Visigoth leader Alaric I, Babur of the Mogul Empire of India, and Gaiseric, the Vandal chieftain. Geographically, the eight rulers included in this book, when taken together, ruled over most of Asia and Europe at different times. They were the leaders of different national and ethnic groups at different levels of civilization. In time span, the eight men's careers ranged over a good deal of the last 2,200 years of human history. In addition, Shih Huang-ti and Muhammad II are interesting and important men who are not as well known to the western world as they should be. Like all such rulers, the eight have much in common, and many differences.

A word needs to be said about the forms of proper names of persons and places used in this book. In the case of the Huns and the Mongols, for example, there is no way of knowing what the pronunciation of a name was. There is also the problem of transcribing names not only from a foreign language but also from a script entirely different from the Latin alphabet, such as Arabic, Chinese and Russian. As Denis Sinor comments in his introduction to René Grousset's *Conqueror of the World:* "Often one is almost tempted to toss a coin to decide on which transcription to adopt."

For example, in addition to the form used here—Jenghiz Khan—I have found five other spellings of the Mongol ruler's name: Chingis, Chinggis, Genghis, Genghiz, and Jengis. Not to mention that some authors use a hyphen between the two parts of the name and some don't! Admitting "I cannot claim any consistency in my transliteration of names from Greek or Turkish," Steven Runciman in *The Fall of Constantinople* lists

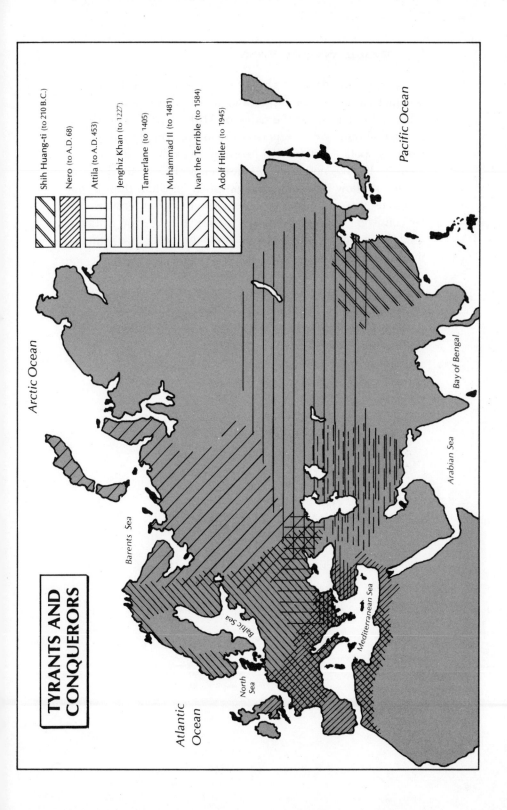

## TYRANTS AND CONQUERORS

Shih Huang-ti (to 210 B.C.)

Nero (to A.D. 68)

Attila (to A.D. 453)

Jenghiz Khan (to 1227)

Tamerlane (to 1405)

Muhammad II (to 1481)

Ivan the Terrible (to 1584)

Adolf Hitler (to 1945)

Arctic Ocean

Pacific Ocean

Atlantic Ocean

Barents Sea

Baltic Sea

North Sea

Mediterranean Sea

Arabian Sea

Bay of Bengal

as possible, in place of the form used here—Muhammad—
Mehmet (which he prefers), Mahomet and Mohammed. Another writer has found the name of Attila's father recorded in
seven different ways. A person begins to feel that the same
name is spelled differently in every book he reads. Consequently, I make no claim to consistency. I have tried on the
whole to follow the most common practice when there is one
and to use the simplest forms of names. I have at least tried to
be consistent within groups of names. I have, for instance,
used the names of Jenghiz Khan's four sons as they are spelled
in the work of one accepted authority.

Finally, there is difficulty in determining the exact dates of
certain events in terms of the calendar of the western world
because scholarly writers do not always agree. But I have tried
to keep straight the order of events and the relationship of
these events to each other.

# Shih Huang-ti: Unity Through Bloodshed

Shih Huang-ti (259–210 B.C.) was the first emperor of a unified China. A superstitious and fear-ridden man, he ruled in arbitrary fashion over one of the world's largest empires and accomplished a great deal in consolidating and improving administration, transportation and communication. Although he built many roads and numerous palaces he was also directly or indirectly responsible for the deaths of hundreds of thousands of soldiers and workers. His reign saw the simplification of the Chinese written language but also witnessed an attempt to burn all the books recording past Chinese history.

The future emperor was born in the northwest state of Ch'in, the state that gave the name China to the whole land. His father may have been Lu Pu-wei, a merchant from Honan in eastern China who moved to Ch'in and became a powerful government official. He succeeded in putting one royal prince of his choice on the throne of Ch'in but, caught in court intrigue, Lu Pu-wei committed suicide by taking poison in 235 B.C.

The history of China began to be recorded about 1500 B.C. Thus there are various sources for knowing what went on before, during and after the short-lived Ch'in dyanasty of which Shih Huang-ti was the founder. The primary source is found in the writings of Ssu-ma Ch'ien (145?–90? B.C.), who is called the father of Chinese history and who was generally unfriendly in his attitude toward the Ch'in. For example, he described the emperor as a "man with a prominent nose, with large eyes, with the chest of a bird of prey, with the face of a jackal; without beneficence, and with the heart of a tiger or a wolf." Ssu-ma Ch'ien was an official at the court of the emperor Wu Ti of the Han dynasty where he wrote his *Shih chi (Memoirs of an Historian)*. He pursued his historical writing even when he fell from the emperor's favor, was castrated and thrown into jail. Ssu-ma Ch'ien wrote about a century after Shih Huang-ti ruled.

Around 4,000 years ago, a generally uniform culture was spreading over China in spite of periods of turbulence and invasion. Traditionally, the first dynasty to rule territory representing China was the Hsia, one of several hundred tribes in northern China. According to later accounts, a Hsia leader named Yu began to rule about 2000 B.C. The first documented dynasty was that of the Shang, a tribe that conquered its neighbor, the Hsia, and exercised some authority over an area of northern China. This dynasty took power about 1523 B.C. and lasted until 1027 or thereabouts. Two extremely important events took place during the Shang period: bronze metallurgy was discovered and a written language was developed.

The Shang dynasty was overthrown by the Chou, a pastoral people who moved south and east from the Wei valley. In a final battle, the unpopular Shang king, Shou, was defeated by King Wu of Chou. The loser set his palace on fire and threw himself into the flames. The dominance of the Chou spread until it took in the area from south Manchuria to parts of the Yangtze valley and from the Kansu region to the Yellow Sea. The Chou regime was feudal in nature, much like that of Medieval Europe. Many lords held lands of varying extent; the higher nobility owed allegiance to the Chou king and the lesser lords to those above them. This system gave the central government less power over local rulers and made it difficult to obtain strict loyalty and obedience.

As a result, by about 800 B.C. the Chou king, in his capital near the present city of Sian, had lost a great deal of authority.

The heads of some states warred with their neighbors and defied the king while they took over more territory. In 771 B.C. the chief of the state of Shen, feeling that the king had insulted him, secured the support of an army of non-Chinese "barbarians" from the west. He attacked the Chou capital, killed the king and forced the government to flee into Honan province. This ended the effective rule of the Chou dynasty although it remained in existence in name for 500 years.

The idea that whoever rules China is the "Son of Heaven," and therefore outranks all other rulers in the world, began under the Chous. They believed that their king was descended from an agricultural deity. This theory of government held that heaven's mandate might be withdrawn from a ruler at any time and this, they said, explained the fall of the Shang king. A ruler should be wise, set a moral example and rule for the benefit of his people. If he was overthrown, he must have ruled unwisely; but if he remained on his throne, he must be ruling properly. Such a point of view also resulted in a Chinese proverb: "He who succeeds becomes emperor; he who fails is a bandit."

The later and troubled years of the Chou dynasty were also the years in which Chinese philosophy and literature were formed through the works of Lao-tze, Confucius and Mencius. It was roughly at this same time that Socrates, Plato and Aristotle were establishing the greatness of Greek philosophy on the other side of the world. Lao-tze, the reputed founder of Taoism, was said to have been born about 604 B.C. According to legends and to Ssu-ma Ch'ien, he was the librarian at the Chou court. In any event, Taoism as a philosophy taught simplicity, passivity and freedom from desire. Transferred to the realm of government, Taoism called for a ruler who would keep his people simple and free from want while imposing a minimum of government on them.

Confucius (c. 551–479? B.C.) was a wandering scholar and founder of a school of thought whose teaching over the centuries became the official doctrine of the Chinese Empire. Confucius deplored the unsettled times in which he lived. His

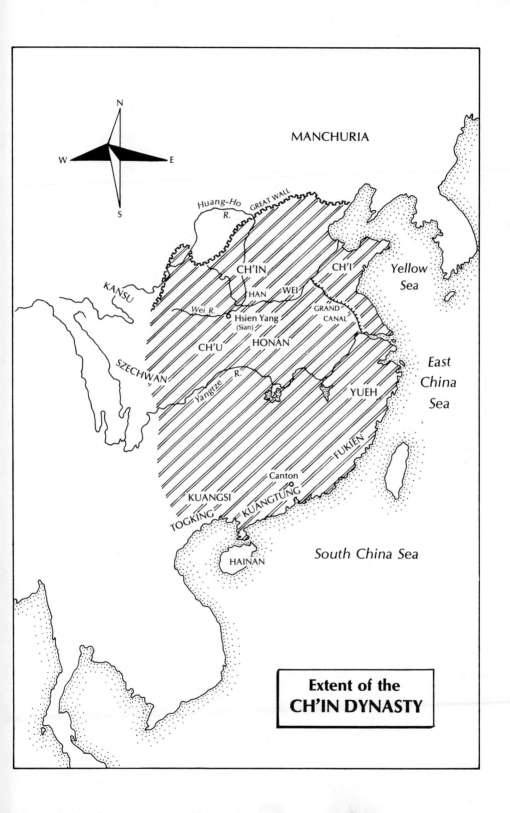

MANCHURIA

Huang-Ho R.

GREAT WALL

CH'IN

CH'I

Yellow Sea

KANSU

HAN

WEI

Wei R.

GRAND CANAL

Hsien Yang (Sian)

CH'U

HONAN

SZECHWAN

Yangtze R.

East China Sea

YUEH

FUKIEN

KUANGSI

Canton

KUANGTUNG

TOGKING

South China Sea

HAINAN

**Extent of the CH'IN DYNASTY**

thought was mostly concerned with relationships within a society and their place in a government and culture that conducted public affairs in an orderly manner. A son should defer to a father and a subject was in the same relationship to the ruler. The ruler, too, must be a moral man, thinking of the welfare of his people and using statesmanship to keep the world stable and peaceful. Confucius never received recognition in the form of government posts while he lived but he was, in the long run, the most influential Chinese of all time.

Born about 100 years after Confucius died, Mencius (371?– 288? B.C.) became the foremost Confucian philosopher and advocate of his day. He, too, was appalled by the warfare of the time. Like Confucius, he believed in the natural goodness of human beings, but said this could either be turned to evil or made better, depending on circumstances. Rulers should not cause the deaths of thousands of their subjects in battle but should avoid warfare and do everything possible to improve the welfare of the people.

In spite of such teachings, the struggle for control among the states of north and central China continued and grew in ferocity. A period known as the Warring States era began in 403 B.C. when one of the larger states, Chin, was thoroughly defeated and divided into three states: Chao, Han and Wei. The other rival states were Ch'in, Ch'i, Ch'u and Yueh, making seven in all. Each sought to dominate because, while all believed China should be unified, each wanted to be the state to do the unifying. Alliances shifted, truces were declared and peace treaties made, but still the fighting went on. In 323 Ch'in and Ch'u agreed to gang up on Ch'i, but four years later Ch'u tried to form an alliance to destroy Ch'in. After 100 years of such strife Ch'in, Ch'i and Ch'u appeared to be about equal and to be ready to divide the country among themselves; but five years later, the Ch'in army captured the Ch'u king.

The long, drawn-out warfare was fought in a country whose population, nevertheless, continued to grow and reached 50,000,000 or more. Some of these people fled the disturbances and so spread Chinese culture over a larger area. At the same time, the warring princes brought in non-Chinese soldiers from outside their borders and they too were exposed to Chinese civilization. They were needed to help make up the huge armies that took the field. The larger states are said to have had as many as 1,000,000 men under arms. These large units had iron weapons and crossbows, arms which were not used in Europe until 1,000 years later. The war chariot, which had been restricted to the noble class, gave way to large units of cavalry. The Chinese of the northwest regions, notably Chao and Ch'in, learned the advantages of mobile horsemen the hard way, by fighting the nomadic steppe people on their borders. The adoption of cavalry also meant that the traditional long-skirted garb of the Chinese had to be abandoned in favor of riding trousers.

The state of Ch'in had some advantages which helped it to become the ultimate victor. The other states, in fact, did not consider the Ch'in to be truly Chinese because their culture was partly Chinese and partly that of the uncivilized steppe society. Probably the people of Ch'in had a good deal of Tatar (a general name for the nomadic tribes) blood in them. They were physically hardy farmers and fierce warriors. Mountains to the south and east protected them from attack, but they could emerge from mountain passes to attack their foes. When they did so, Ssu-ma Ch'ien said, "It was like a man emptying a jug of water from the top of a high house." Ch'in has been compared to Macedon, the area of northern Greece which was looked down on by the more civilized city-states south of it, but out of which during this same era (the fourth century B.C.) came the father and son conquerors Philip II and Alexander the Great.

The state of Ch'in was also fortunate in having energetic rulers and unusually competent statesmen in charge of its affairs in the era of the Warring States. Notable among the officials was Shang Yang, who was chief minister from 361 until his death in 338 B.C. He introduced new forms of taxation and favored the military leaders over the old aristocracy. The rules he enforced were harsh, such as: "Anyone who does not denounce a culprit will be cut in two at the waist." The man who was soon to be emperor of all China became the ruler of Ch'in in 247, when he was only twelve years old. His name then was King Cheng, and he was an energetic and ambitious leader who led Ch'in to victory over its rival states.

In the course of the first three quarters of the third century B.C., Ch'in eliminated all its rival states in the most brutal kind of warfare. The army of Wei met defeat in 274 and 150,000 of its troops were killed. An even greater slaughter took place in 260 B.C. when the army of Chao was routed and 400,000 soldiers were reportedly massacred. King Nan of Chou, still claiming the title of ruler of all China, was defeated in 256 and the Chou dynasty came to an end. By about 230 B.C., Ch'in controlled a third of all the cultivated land and population of China. Between then and 221, the rival states were completely defeated, Ch'i being the last to fall. King Sheng, who had efficiently if callously led the Ch'in triumphs of the last quarter century, was supreme over the empire. Ssu-ma Ch'ien commented that the victors had absorbed the other states "as a silkworm devours the mulberry leaf."

In 221 B.C. the Ch'in dynasty became the first to establish effective rule over China. King Cheng, who loved anything that attested to his grandeur, took the title of Shih Huang-ti (sometimes written with *Ch'in* in front of it), or First Emperor. He decreed that his successors should be known as Second Emperor, and so on, "until thousands of generations to come." The emperor in 219 journeyed to T'ai Shan, the sacred mountain of Shantung, where he declared he received a mandate from heaven "to rule all that is on earth." The Ch'in were on top by virtue of warfare and the emperor's ego was inflated by his exalted position, but it is likely that most Chinese welcomed his rule after centuries of warfare.

The China of the Ch'ins extended from southern Manchuria to northern Vietnam (after some further conquests) and from the East China Sea to the eastern slopes of the Tibetan plateau—one of the largest governmental units the world has known. China has a great variety of soils, valleys and mountains and two of the largest river systems, the Huang Ho (or Yellow) River in the north and the Yangtze River in central China. The soil in much of the agricultural areas is loess, or fine-grained, yellowish minerals mixed with clay. The Ch'in established their capital at Hsien Yang, near the site of the present-day city of Sian in Shensi province.

In theory and practice, Shih Huang-ti and Ch'in accepted the idea of a mandate to the Son of Heaven, and the belief that China should be united by such a ruler. The Ch'in also accepted the common belief that it was the government's duty to preserve internal peace and order, to see to the welfare of the citizens and to look out for the morals of the nation as well. However, the Ch'in methods for achieving these goals were not in accordance with Taoism or Confucianism, which set forth ideals of minimum government, simplicity of life and the natural goodness of man. Rather, Shih Huang-ti put into practice the ideas of the Legalists, who placed the absolute power and the centralized administration of the state above all else.

As a theory of government, Legalism was first expressed in writing in the fourth century B.C. and developed in the next century when it was put into practice under the Ch'in dynasty. Legalism assumed that mankind was bad and had to be ruled firmly, with strict punishments as well as rewards. Agriculture was favored over trade and scholarship because it was, according to the Legalists, the only true source of a nation's wealth. The state was justified in using any means necessary to carry out its policies and to keep itself strong. Legalism was rational and recognized the necessity of increasing the material welfare of the people, but it was also without moral values and was totalitarian to an extreme.

In the third century B.C., two men took Legalism a few steps further, one by his writings, the other in practice as a government official. Han Fei was sent in 234 B.C. by Ch'in's enemy state of Han to negotiate with King Cheng, but he seems to have defected. He was the author of *Han Fei Tzu*, which he wrote as a guide to government for his Han king. Han Fei was jailed in Ch'in in 233 and forced to commit suicide. The official responsible was Li Ssu (280?–208 B.C.), who had been Han Fei's schoolmate when they studied together under a leading teacher of Confucianism, but who was apparently jealous of Han Fei's influence.

Li Ssu, a native of the state of Ch'u, arrived in Ch'in in 247 B.C. It was a common practice for members of the lower nobility and even some men of more humble origin to secure an education in order to become government officials. Members of ruling families often concentrated on military matters and had little formal education. They therefore needed educated men. It was also common practice to go from state to state seeking government posts without regard to whether one was serving one's native state or not. Li Ssu became a senior scribe in Ch'in and was promoted to minister of justice in 237 when he convinced King Cheng to withdraw an edict that would have expelled all aliens from Ch'in, thus depriving the state of their services and the taxes they paid. When the king became emperor in 221, Li Ssu was appointed grand councillor and remained the chief minister of the empire until his death. Credit or blame for many of the actions of Shih Huang-ti belong to Li Ssu. The emperor was basically a warrior, uncultured and given to impetuous actions. Li Ssu, on the other hand, practiced in extreme form the authoritarian theories of the Legalists. His only concern was the power of the state and he was, probably, as much the unifier of China as was the emperor.

The Ch'in dynasty established the Chinese Empire on a new foundation, one that lasted with no basic change, under various dynasties, until 1912. Feudalism was abolished; no longer did hereditary lords rule their fiefs almost independently. Instead, China was divided into 36 commanderies (later increased to 42) with a military governor and a civil administrator in charge of each. All officials were responsible to the administrators directly above them, up to the central government and Li Ssu. Government appointments were made on the basis of ability and merit. The dynasty formed and trained a professional standing army that could be kept in readiness at all times and it was no longer dependent on the troops each feudal lord was expected to supply under the old system.

The farming population was freed of its subservience to feudal lords of the manor and became peasants with their own land or tenant farmers. But the practical gain for them was slight. Very heavy taxes were imposed by the Ch'in regime and the men were subject to both military service and forced labor on roads and other public projects. Merchants and others such as vagabonds were deported to distant areas to populate the land. The criminal laws were extremely severe. A family was punished for the wrongdoing of one of its members; if a family got into trouble, its neighbors often suffered, too. Punishments included mutilation, execution, branding on the top of the head, extracting ribs and boiling in a cauldron.

As part of the drive to standardize everything in accordance with Legalist philosophy, the regime reformed the currency. Prior to the Ch'in dynasty, there were many kinds of coins with wide variation in value. Under the emperor, two kinds of currency were established: gold, used by the upper classes; and bronze coins weighing half an ounce. The bronze coins were round with square holes in their centers so they could be strung on a cord.

As soon as he was on the throne, Shih Huang-ti had all weapons belonging to the feudal lords seized. Any not needed were melted down and cast into bells and into a dozen gigantic human figures to adorn the imperial palace. Fortifications the nobles had erected in their territories were destroyed. In the most radical step of all, the emperor forced 120,000 nobles to move from their own lands to the capital city where they would be without supporters or other facilities for causing trouble. To compensate them, and to take some of the sting out of the forced migration, Shih Huang-ti erected for each of them a palace just like the one the nobleman had been forced to abandon. This project, no doubt, caused a great deal of forced labor on the part of the lower class. The emperor also bestowed honorary titles on the powerless feudal nobles.

Shih Huang-ti survived three attempts to assassinate him, the first time in 227 when he was still King Cheng. A man named Ching K'o was sent by the state of Yen as the era of Warring States neared its end. He came very close to succeeding but was seized and cut to pieces. "The king of Ch'in," says Ssu-ma Ch'ien, "was not at ease for a long time." Soon after the unification of the empire, a friend of Ching K'o, who was able to get close to the emperor because he was a court musician, made another attempt. Of this the historian wrote that Shih Huang-ti "to the end of his life did not again allow followers of the feudal lords to come close to him." The final attempt at assassination came in 218. It was made by a native of Han, Chang Liang, who was trying to avenge the conquest of his native state. Chang Liang sought to kill the emperor while an imperial procession passed by, but he attacked the wrong chariot.

Shih Huang-ti was a brave general but he was very superstitious and had a great fear of death. To be superstitious was common and anyone who had escaped three assassination attempts might well fear death at any time. The emperor tried to protect himself with court magicians and astrologers, and he became obsessed with a search for an elixir that would make him immortal. Hearing that in the sea to the east there were supernatural mountains on which dwelled immortal beings, he sent one of his magicians to find them and bring back the secret of eternal life. The magician was accompanied by several thousand boys and girls. The expedition never returned, which led to the legend that the young people reached Japan and became the first settlers there from the mainland. Again in 215 Shih Huang-ti sent three men in search of the elixir, but they failed to find it.

Like several other absolute monarchs, Shih Huang-ti built palaces on the grandest scale possible. He is said to have had 270 within a radius of about 60 miles, and they were all connected by covered roads or roads with walls on each side. According to a poet of a later time, the emperor's palaces "block out the skies for more than 300 *li.*" (A *li* was about a third of a mile.) The largest, Afang Palace, designed to seat 10,000 people, measured 2,500 feet from east to west and 500 feet from north to south. The forced labor of 700,000 people was required to build this residence. Shih Huang-ti lived an aloof and carefully guarded life within the royal residences. He moved from one to another because of his fear of death, and only a handful of officials knew where he was at any given time. Nevertheless, he had a reputation as a very hard worker, dealing every day with 120 pounds of reports written on strips of wood and bamboo.

The Ch'in dynasty began a large-scale road-building program in 220, constructing highways 50 paces wide and lined with trees. They led to all parts of the empire and converged on the capital. In addition, the gauge of the wheels of carts was ordered to be the same all over the land so that they could run easily in the ruts that they cut into the roads' soft soil. The splendid road system was useful for moving troops, for inspections and for gathering information. The emperor spent a great deal of time traveling to almost every part of his realm. While on these journeys he erected tablets along the way with inscriptions on them, such as: "For the first time he has united the world," or, "The Sovereign Emperor has pacified in turn the four ends of the earth." Li Ssu, who claimed credit for planning the system of highways, may have been the one who composed the inscriptions.

Under Shih Huang-ti, canals and irrigation systems were also constructed. One canal, connecting a tributary of the Yangtze River to rivers that flow south, was very useful in transporting supplies to the Ch'in army when it fought in southern China. Measures of weight, of capacity and of size were standardized, and for this Li Ssu again took credit.

For years before unification, the various states, especially those in the north of China, had built walls many miles in length as protection against their neighbors and the uncivilized tribes of the steppes. As soon as he became emperor, Shih Huang-ti sent one of his leading generals, Meng T'ien, with 300,000 peasants and soldiers to the north. His orders were to link the various walls previously built by individual states into one powerful line of defense that would keep out the northern barbarians. It is said that Meng T'ien carried out his assignment at the cost of 1,000,000 lives. Many of those who died while doing the work were buried within the walls. Thus, under the Ch'in dynasty, the Great Wall of China ran about 1,500 miles from Kansu in the west to the sea in Manchuria. The nomadic barbarians Shih Huang-ti sought to keep out of China by forming the Great Wall were known to the Chinese as the Hsiung-nu and were probably the same people Europe called the Huns when they invaded that continent nearly 600 years later.

Between 221 and 214 B.C. the Ch'in dynasty extended its rule over southern China, conquering the regions of Fukien, Kuangtung, Kuangsi and Togking. These victories included the occupation of the largest southern city, Canton, in 214.

A lasting and important achievement was the standardization and simplification of the written language, for which Li Ssu deserves credit rather than Shih Huang-ti. Over the centuries the very complex written language of China had developed along different lines in different states so that by the time of the Ch'in unification much that was written in one place was unintelligible elsewhere. Taking the Ch'in style as a model, Li Ssu decreed a modified form of script that became known as the Small Seal and which the regime imposed on all of China. This reform, perhaps the most important accomplishment of the Ch'in dynasty, set a standard for all Chinese writing thereafter and helped promote the development of a national literature.

An event of 213, also inspired by Li Ssu, was not as beneficial, however. He proposed a plan, approved by the emperor, for burning all the books containing the history of other states and rulers so that the Ch'in dynasty would stand alone and without comparison. The Ch'in were not the first

Chinese ruling group to attempt to erase history, but they applied the torch on a larger scale. A great many books were destroyed, although part of the plan called for retaining at least one copy of each title, and books on technology, medicine and divination were exempt. The scheme was intended to give the regime a monopoly on learning, not only in history but also in literature. A considerable number of the banned books escaped the flames, but an even greater loss to history and learning occurred in 206 when the emperor's palace and its library were burned during the overthrow of the dynasty. One book of history from the early Chou era was retrieved in later years when a 90-year-old Confucian scholar, who had memorized the entire text, dictated it to his daughter.

The next year the Ch'in effort to control history and intellectual activity was extended to the scholars of the empire. Shih Huang-ti would not allow any dissent from his own ideas and laws for fear it would disturb the government's control of the land and the people. Accordingly, 460 scholars, some of whom were more magicians and astrologers than true scholars, were accused of slandering the emperor. They were also alleged to have "spread heretical ideas to confuse the public." Shih Huang-ti had them buried alive, and ordered other scholars in the provinces sent to the frontiers as soldiers. When Fu-su, the eldest of the emperor's many sons, protested, he was exiled to serve with General Meng T'ien in the far north.

Shih Huang-ti went on another tour of his kingdom in 210, visiting the eastern seacoast, partly as an inspection and partly as another futile search for the elixir that would allow him to live forever. He had been told by his magicians that a very large fish had prevented earlier attempts to reach the islands where the immortals lived. On the trip the emperor saw a large fish and killed it with his crossbow, but shortly afterwards he fell ill and died. The officials with him wished to keep his death a secret until they could get back to the capital to make certain they controlled the events surrounding the succession to the throne. They had servants serve food in his chariot, as though the emperor were alive, but during the long journey in hot weather Shih Huang-ti's body decomposed so badly that the ministers placed a carload of spoiled fish next to his chariot to hide the fact that he was dead.

The emperor had secretly begun construction of his tomb while he was still alive. Ssu-ma Ch'ien later described it:

> He employed his soldiery . . . to bore down to the Three Springs and there a foundation of bronze was laid and the sarcophagus placed thereon. Rare objects and costly jewels were collected from the palaces and from the various officials, and were carried thither and stored in vast quantities. Artificers were ordered to construct mechanical crossbows, which if anyone were to enter, would immediately discharge their arrows. With the aid of quicksilver, rivers were made . . . and a great ocean, the metal being poured from one into the other by machinery. On the roof were delineated the constellations of the sky, on the floor the geographical divisions of the earth.

All the emperor's concubines who had no children were killed and buried with him. When the workmen who entombed him finsihed their work, they found the exit closed, and they perished, too. The tomb was covered with earth, and planted with trees and grass; the whole effect was of a hill 550 feet high.

Li Ssu was on the tour with the emperor when he died and so was Chao Kao, whose title was keeper of the chariots. Chao Kao was also in charge of sending out letters and orders on the emperor's behalf and was the next most important official after Li Ssu. Before he died, Shih Huang-ti gave the two men orders to write to his son Fu-su to return from Meng T'ien's commandery to become crown prince and his eventual successor. Li Ssu and Chao Kao decided they would retain more power and prestige if Shih Huang-ti were succeeded by his second son, Hu-hai, a weak-willed young man who was interested mainly in enjoying himself. The two officials sent off a letter to Fu-su and Meng T'ien in the emperor's name, blaming them for lack of military success and ordering them both to commit suicide. The son accepted what he thought was his father's wish and killed himself, but the general refused and was imprisoned.

Chao Kao, promoted to palace chamberlain, became more influential than Li Ssu. He poisoned the mind of Hu-hai, who had taken the title of Erh-shih Huang-ti, or second emperor, and who proceeded to have twelve of the royal princes murdered. Ten royal princesses also died by being torn limb from limb. The new emperor's rule was even harsher than his father's and more erratic. He ordered larger numbers of men to do forced labor and great numbers of people to be tortured or killed. Chao Kao intrigued successfully against Li Ssu, who, while a believer in the harsh practices of Legalism, did execute his duties honorably. He thereby made the new emperor suspicious of him. Li Ssu was arrested and jailed and given a flogging of more than a thousand strokes. In the summer of 208 B.C. he was executed by being cut in two at the waist. All his family were killed also.

Armed revolt against the Ch'in dynasty began a year after Shih Huang-ti's death in 209, and was triggered by the harsh laws of the regime. Two leaders of a group of 900 peasants were late in getting the men to the place where they were to perform forced labor. Rains had made the roads impassable, but no excuses were accepted. The only punishment was death. The two leaders, Chen Sheng and Wu Kuang, decided they might as well revolt. This they did, and they were soon joined by many more peasants and other fugitives from the law of the empire. Dispossessed feudal lords also revolted, as did the members of families of past rulers in Ch'in's rival states. Chen Sheng was elected head of the peasant movement but he was not favored by the nobles, who formed their own government. Chen Sheng was treacherously murdered. In the

course of these events, in 207 B.C., Chao Kao, still intriguing
for supreme power, had Erh-shih Huang-ti put to death and
planned to place his nephew, Ying, on the throne.

Before he could do this, however, the Ch'in dynasty fell.
The eventually successful leader of the revolt was Liu Pang, a
minor official of peasant origin, who defeated other rival
revolutionists. Rebel forces captured the Ch'in capital city
Hsien Yang, killed the members of the royal family and set fire
to all the palaces. And so the Ch'in dynasty came to an end in
ruins in 206 B.C. Liu Pang won supremacy over his last rival in
202 B.C. and the new Han dynasty is dated from that year. He
became emperor as Han Kao-tsu and set about changing the
laws of the empire in certain respects. The feudal system was
resumed but in modified form so that the Han rulers could
keep close control of the nobles. Harsh laws were modified,
taxes were reduced and, most important of all, the theories of
Confucianism replaced those of the Legalists. The Han
dynasty, except for an interruption of 14 years, lasted until
A.D. 220, a period of four centuries.

Compared with the rest of the world at that time, the Ch'in
dynasty was enormously successful, although short-lived. In
this same period, Rome and Carthage fought the Second Punic
War (218–201 B.C.), from which Carthage never recovered,
and which helped make Rome the only other empire in the
world comparable in size to the newly unified Chinese
Empire. For this unification was vital, even though it was
brought about by bloodshed, if China was to become a great
nation culturally as well as politically. And in bringing this
about, Shih Huang-ti and the Ch'in state affected the future
not only of China but also of the rest of the world. The
harshness of some of the dynasty's laws and the brutality of its
methods in such matters as burning books and burying men
alive were in part offset by other actions it took, such as the
standardization of the written language and the building of
roads and canals.

In the same way, Shih Huang-ti was neither wholly good
nor wholly bad. He was an efficient but uncultured warrior,

but so were most rulers of the time. He was a military leader in an era when to be one meant to fight one's enemies continually for supremacy or be destroyed. He sought conquest for survival, power and prestige, and it is doubtful he had the long-range good of the Chinese people in mind when he led Ch'in to the victory that caused him to be acclaimed the unifier of China. Yet he did see—or came to see through his advisers—the national benefits that could be achieved by unified efforts and by laws and policies applied to the whole country.

# Nero: The Tyrant as Coward

The Emperor Nero (A.D. 37–68) ruled for fourteen years with almost unlimited power over the Roman Empire. It was then at the height of its glory and one of the most durable and extensive empires in the history of the world. Nero cold-bloodedly had his mother, one wife, and other relatives and associates murdered; he kicked another wife to death; and burned Christians as human torches. He finally committed suicide when threatened by death at the hands of some of the enemies he had made.

Nero was born Lucius Domitius Ahenobarbus at Anzio, Italy, on December 15, A.D. 37. His father, Gnaeus Domitius Ahenobarbus, was, as one historian has written, "a wholly despicable character." He drank heavily and was eventually imprisoned for treason. Nero's mother was Julia Agrippina the Younger (A.D. 15–59), so called because her mother was also named Agrippina. An ambitious schemer all her life, she was the granddaughter of the first emperor, Augustus, and the daughter of Nero Claudius Germanicus (15 B.C.–A.D. 19), a Roman general and hero. Her brother was Caligula, another notoriously corrupt emperor. When Nero was three, his father died, and Caligula not only seized the third of his property that should have gone to Nero, but also banished Agrippina from Rome.

For a while Nero lived with an aunt in rather squalid circumstances but when Claudius (10 B.C.–A.D. 54), brother of Germanicus, succeeded Caligula as emperor in 41, Nero's life changed. Claudius restored Nero's fortune and recalled Agrippina from banishment and married her. The Roman Senate changed the law so that he could marry his niece. Claudius's previous wife, Valeria Messalina (A.D. 24–48), whose lust was said to be insatiable and who was suspected of being involved in a plot to displace Claudius, was executed. She was the mother of Britannicus (A.D 41?–55) and Octavia (A.D. 40?–62). Agrippina set about to make Claudius, who was weak-willed and easily influenced, favor her son over Britannicus. She won a major victory when in February, 50, Claudius adopted the boy who became known as Nero Claudius Caesar Augustus Germanicus.

The emperor's new son was given excellent tutors, mostly Greek, but when he showed too much interest in philosophy and other of the liberal arts, his mother intervened on the grounds that these were not subjects suitable for a future emperor, which she was determined he should be. Agrippina took every advantage of the fact that her son was a few years older than Britannicus to push him forward. Usually, Roman boys assumed the *toga virilis*, the dress that indicated they were adults, when they reached the age of fourteen, but Nero appeared in public so garbed before this. He could now enter public life. The Senate, mindful of the fact that he was the great-grandson of the deified Augustus, and sensing that he was to be the chosen heir of Claudius, voted that he should hold the office of consul, the Senate's highest honor, when he became twenty. In the meantime, he was termed Prince of Youth and wore suitable robes at public games where Britannicus appeared in the costume of a minor.

The Emperor Claudius died on October 13, A.D. 54, after being taken violently ill at dinner. A number of stories are told about the cause of his death, but it is most likely that he was poisoned at the instigation of Agrippina. She hired a well-known concocter of poisons, a woman named Locusta, to prepare a dish of poisoned mushrooms, although some accounts say Claudius vomited this up and had to be poisoned a second time. In any event, Agrippina, knowing there was no

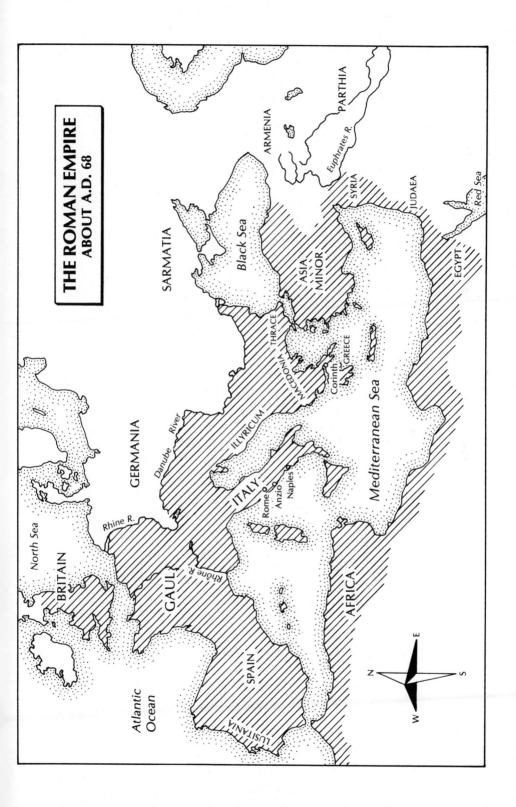

THE ROMAN EMPIRE
ABOUT A.D. 68

PARTHIA

ARMENIA

Euphrates R.

SYRIA

JUDAEA

Red Sea

EGYPT

ASIA
MINOR

Black Sea

SARMATIA

THRACE

MACEDONIA

GREECE

Corinth

ILLYRICUM

Danube River

GERMANIA

ITALY

Rome
Anzio
Naples

Rhine R.

Rhône R.

GAUL

North Sea

BRITAIN

Atlantic
Ocean

SPAIN

LUSITANIA

AFRICA

Mediterranean Sea

N
E
W
S

automatic succession to the throne, saw to it that Claudius's death was kept secret for some hours, and that Britannicus was held inside the palace until all her plans were completed. Then Nero was led out, escorted by the commander of the Praetorian Guard, to be welcomed by the soldiers on duty who proclaimed him emperor.

The seventeen-year-old emperor was taken to the Praetorian Guard's camp where, as was the custom, he promised them a sum of money. Claudius was deified, the first emperor to receive this honor since Augustus, and Nero delivered an oration at his funeral. It was, incidentally, the first time a Roman ruler had employed a speech writer to prepare his words for him. Nero praised Claudius, although some laughed when he referred to the late ruler's foresight and wisdom. He promised the Senate he would show no favoritism and would keep his personal and public affairs separate.

Both contemporary observers and later historians pay more attention to Nero's flamboyant private life than to his official acts. The contemporary accounts have not survived but we have the works of later historians who had to rely for the most part on these earlier writings. As a result, we see Nero chiefly through unsympathetic eyes. In addition, the ruling upper-class Romans were a very permissive society, so Nero's debauched style of private life, his cruelty, and his arbitrary official acts were not considered unusual.

Three historians through whose eyes we see Nero today were Cornelius Tacitus (c. 55–c.117), Gaius Suetonius Tranquillus (c. 69–c.140) and Dio Cassius (c. 155–235). Tacitus was the only one of the three who lived during Nero's reign but he did not write his *Annals* until nearly fifty years after the emperor died. Tacitus held high government positions and so was familiar with the workings of the empire. His writings are mostly reliable but written in a tone of longing for "the good old days" when, he thought, men were more virtuous. Suetonius gathered some of his material for *The Twelve Caesars* from eye witnesses, but he is not as reliable as Tacitus. He served for a while as chief secretary to the Emperor

Hadrian, but was dismissed by him in 121. Dio Cassius served in the Senate and also held the office of consul. He wrote eighty books of Roman history, of which only about a quarter have survived in full. Dio was an earnest seeker of facts and had a skeptical attitude toward his subject.

The young emperor, who was to grow into a monster in the eyes of the historians, was of average height and his eyes, Suetonius records, were "dullish blue." He had spindly legs and as he grew older his stomach protruded noticeably; this was not surprising, considering the way he indulged himself. Nero's hair was light blond and usually arranged in curls, although when he went to Greece in 66 he let it grow long and hang down his back. He had a bull neck and this is shown realistically on Roman coins, which, along with statues, provide the modern world with portraits of the emperor.

Nero's family fortune was very large, consisting mainly of land on which thousands of slaves were employed, but it also included such businesses as a tile factory in conquered Britain. The wealth of the imperial family increased regularly because it was the custom for members of the upper class to leave part of their estates to the emperor. In addition, the estates of criminals, especially those executed for treason, were usually confiscated. Since the emperor also had almost complete control over the public treasury, the wealth at his disposal was enormous.

At the beginning of his reign, Nero was fortunate to have two able men as his advisers and administrators. They were Lucius Annaeus Seneca (c. 38 B.C.–A.D. 65) and Sextus Afranius Burrus (d. 62). Seneca was born in Spain of a wealthy family and studied philosophy in Rome before becoming tutor to Nero in A.D. 49. He wrote philosophical essays and tragedies in verse, as well as the oration Nero delivered at Claudius's funeral. Despite the high moral tone of his philosophical works, Seneca attempted to amass as large a fortune as possible, with the assistance of the emperor. It was said that he owned five hundred identical tables with ivory legs.

Burrus had been appointed commander of the Praetorian

Guard by Claudius in 51 and continued to hold the post under Nero. This elite unit of the Roman army had been formed by Augustus as the emperor's bodyguard and had grown in size and power ever since. Its members had special privileges and every emperor was careful to stay in the Guard's good graces by offering presents of money and other favors.

The great empire of Nero's day traced its beginnings to the founding of the city of Rome, which by tradition occurred in 753 B.C. Over the centuries the Roman Republic expanded by force of arms and, under Augustus (63 B.C.–A.D. 14), became an empire. *Augustus* was a title meaning august, or reverend, which the Roman Senate conferred on a leader and general named Octavian. He was the grandson of the sister of Julius Caesar, an earlier Roman general and statesman, one of the most dynamic figures in the rise of Rome to world power. Augustus also held the title of *princeps,* which had come to mean not just a leader but *the* leader. The imperial regime was therefore referred to as the principate. In effect, an imperial regime and a ruling house had been established, but the oldest son did not automatically succeed his father. As a result, the history of the empire became in part a story of bloody intrigue and violent deeds done to claw one's way to the top.

Officially, the Senate remained the supreme legislative body of the empire. Membership was partly by inheritance, but new members were brought in from time to time from among outstanding men who performed public services. The Senate elected two consuls each year and they were, in theory, the highest officials of the state. The Senate, though, usually did whatever the emperors wished and the emperors had a large say in selecting the consuls. Nero, in fact, served five times as consul. Nevertheless, the emperor always made a pretense of consulting the Senate. Under this somewhat uneasy arrangement, Nero ruled an empire that had absorbed Asia Minor and the lands at the eastern end of the Mediterranean Sea; North Africa, including Egypt; all of Europe west of the Rhine and Danube rivers; and southern and eastern England.

Under the guidance of Seneca and Burrus, Nero's first years

were marked by careful and enlightened administration of the affairs of an empire that was no longer dynamic and growing. He presided over law cases and insisted on writing out his decisions instead of simply giving them orally. The coinage of his realm which, as was customary, carried his likeness, was of excellent design. The citizens of Rome were favorably impressed by Nero's efforts to see that the grain supply of the city was maintained. This was no small task since about 7,000,000 bushels had to be imported every year, mostly from North Africa and Sicily. One year, Nero proposed that all indirect taxes in the empire be abolished but he was talked out of the idea because no one could predict the effect on the public revenue. In the later years of his reign, public finance was in poor condition, largely because of expensive public works projects which he had begun.

In the past, most of the men who achieved the highest positions in the republic and the empire had been military heroes. Nero was most unwarlike and never even visited his legions stationed in the various provinces. The governors and generals he appointed were on the whole successful and he left the defense of the realm to them. Two of the three military engagements of his reign were resolved favorably, while the third continued after his death.

The first war of Nero's regime broke out in England, the southeastern part of which had been conquered by 48. Ten years later, the Romans decided to annex more of the island, and the peace-loving emperor agreed because it appeared to be an easy conquest that would bring him favorable publicity at home. The Roman governor of Britain, Suetonius Paulinus (d. after 69), invaded the island of Anglesey, off the northwest coast of Wales, because it was the headquarters of the Druids, priests who worshipped nature deities and who were fiercely anti-Roman. While the Roman general was thus engaged, a revolt broke out in East Anglia, on the other side of England, where the king of the Iceni had recently died. He had accepted Roman supervision, but wished his two daughters to inherit his kingdom. The Romans decided to seize the territory of the Iceni. Soldiers raped the king's daughters and flogged his widow, Boudicca (often, but incorrectly, called Boadicea), condescendingly described by Dio as "possessed of greater intelligence than often belongs to women."

She raised an army said to number 120,000 and while the Roman legions were away in the west, her soldiers captured and sacked Colchester, St. Albans and London. About 70,000 Romans and Romanized Britons were slaughtered. The Roman army, however, rallied and in a final battle defeated Boudicca in 61. According to Tacitus, she took poison, but Dio says she simply fell ill and died.

Rome also came into conflict with the Parthian Empire, the only independent power of consequence whose borders met those of the Romans. The Parthians ruled an area of Asia, south and east of the Caspian Sea, between the Euphrates and Indus rivers. Both Parthia and Rome sought to dominate Armenia, which lay in eastern Asia Minor between the two powers, but they did not want to fight a major war. Nero sent Gnaeus Domitius Corbulo, a successful commander, to Syria, the neighboring Roman province, and in 59 he drove King Tiridates from the Armenian throne in the course of his campaign against Parthia.

Tiridates had been placed in power by his brother, Vologeses I, king of Parthia. The Romans had no real objection to Tiridates if he could convince them he would remain neutral between the Romans and the Parthians. He succeeded in winning the support of Nero when he made a pilgrimage to Rome in 66 and humbly accepted the Armenian crown from him. After a nine-month trip that cost the Roman treasury a fortune, Tiridates arrived with 3,000 cavalrymen and other supporters. Nero staged a gaudy public celebration in Tiridates' honor for which he received much praise, because the Roman public loved a display of this kind. Nero's handling of the Armenian affair was noteworthy for the way he avoided a long and costly war with Parthia.

In the province of Judaea, an uneasy peace existed between the Jewish population and the Roman rulers. This peace was shattered in 66 when the Roman prefect seized some money in the temple treasury in Jerusalem in payment of taxes he said were overdue. Riots broke out and, in retaliation, Roman soldiers were allowed to plunder part of the city. This action led to a full-scale uprising by the Jews and the massacre of Roman inhabitants of the city. In early 67, Nero sent a general, Titus Flavius Vespasianus to Judaea to quell the revolt. The commander, who later became the Emperor Vespasian, was from a poor family but had made a brilliant record as a military leader. The only blot on his record, and one which at the time had nearly cost him his life, was the fact that he had once fallen asleep in a theater while the Emperor Nero was performing. Vespasian's forces moved south from Syria, retook a number of cities and fortresses and were preparing to attack Jerusalem when word of Nero's death reached them in 68.

Nero is remembered, however, not for such events as occurred in the empire but for his personal life. One of the most shocking incidents in it came when he ordered his mother murdered. Agrippina was, if possible, even more monstrous than her son. She arranged the death of a woman who, she thought, wanted to replace her as Claudius's wife; she had M. Junius Silanus killed because he was a great-great-grandson of Augustus and might stand in Nero's way to the throne. A tutor of her stepson, Britannicus, was killed and the latter deprived of further education and held a virtual prisoner in the palace. After Nero's accession, Agrippina urged him to be an active administrator and fancied herself as co-ruler. In this she was strongly opposed by Seneca and Burrus, who forced her to remain behind a curtain, where she could still hear what went on when Nero received ambassadors and carried on other imperial business.

As time passed, Nero formed his own close associations, with both men and women, and began to shake off his mother's influence. This situation caused Agrippina to intrigue all the more, in some cases with those she previously had plotted against. Nero took away her guard in 55 and moved her from the palace into a separate residence. Later, Nero was told of a plot against him fomented by his mother, but she defended herself successfully. Nevertheless, in 59 Nero decided Agrippina must die so he would be free of her lingering influence. With Anicetus, a freedman (a non-Roman who had been a slave) who had tutored Nero and was now a naval officer, Nero devised a scheme for drowning Agrippina in the Bay of Naples. A boat was constructed that not only would split apart at the right time but also had a heavy lead cabin roof that would collapse, it was hoped, onto her head. The "accident" took place, but Agrippina escaped and swam ashore. In a panic, Nero sent Anicetus and some sailors to his mother's home, where they stabbed her to death. Nero did not sleep well for some time after this, and a number of strange events occurred, such as lightning striking the emperor's dinner, that were considered evil omens. About this same time, Nero poisoned his Aunt Domitia, who had cared for him when he was small, so that he could seize her estate.

Four years before his mother's murder, Nero rid himself of his step-brother Britannicus, employing the poisoner Locusta for the purpose. The poison was given to Britannicus in a drink when he, Nero and other noble young men were dining. Nero claimed he died of an epileptic seizure, but plans had been made even before his death for a simple funeral. The gods, it was said, showed their fury by unleashing a violent storm while Britannicus's body was being placed in the imperial tomb.

Nero's married life and the fate of his wives were in keeping with the side of his personality he showed in his relations with his mother. He first married Claudius's daughter Octavia, then only thirteen, in 53, the year before he succeeded her father as emperor. The marriage was arranged by Agrippina but Octavia, a respectable, old-fashioned woman, had little appeal for the pleasure-loving Nero. Another wedge was driven between Nero and his mother in 55 when he took as his mistress a young freedwoman from Asia, Acte. Three years later he became a close companion of Poppaea Sabina, the wife of Marcus Salvius Otho (32–69), a friend whom he appointed governor of a distant province to get him out of the way. Poppaea fought Agrippina's influence and in some quarters was said to have been the one who instigated Agrippina's murder.

Nero's infatuation with Poppaea, and her ambition to be the emperor's wife, caused Nero to get rid of Octavia. He divorced her in 62, on the grounds that she was unable to bear children, after her reputation had been smeared by false charges of adultery which Poppaea arranged. Octavia's downfall was also hastened by the death in 62 of Burrus, who had been her champion. Burrus apparently had cancer of the throat but it is likely that Nero speeded his end with poison. His death further damaged the principate for it weakened Seneca's position and Burrus's successors were not as honorable as he.

The twenty-year-old Octavia, who had never had much happiness out of life, was banished to southern Italy and shortly after was ordered killed by Nero. Her head was cut off and sent to Poppaea. Until now Nero had been quite popular with the public but Octavia, an upright representative of the imperial family, had been much respected, and her death cost Nero some of his popularity. Nero married Poppaea just twelve days after divorcing Octavia. Poppaea gave birth to a daughter on January 21, 63, an event which caused much private and public rejoicing. The baby, however, died after four months. She was declared a goddess and Tacitus later wrote that Nero's "delight had been immoderate; so was his mourning." Poppaea was pregnant again in 65 when one day Nero kicked her in a fit of temper and she died. He never had another child.

Nero's last wife was Statilia Messalina, although he did not marry her until after he had had another woman put to death for refusing his offer of marriage. The official charge against her was conspiracy. He married Messalina in 66, after the execution of her fourth husband for treason. (Divorce and death by execution or forced suicide were frequent among the

Roman upper class. Forced suicide, in fact, was considered more honorable than the indignity of execution.) Messalina survived Nero and, noted for her beauty, eloquence and literary culture, held a brilliant social position.

Nero took time from his marital affairs and official functions to lead a busy and debauched private life. Luxury and extravagance were everywhere: he never wore the same robe twice, his fish nets were made of gold, and Poppaea's mules wore gilded shoes. Nero's banquets with his friends often lasted from noon to midnight. On one such occasion he went through a wedding ceremony with a eunuch whom he then took out in public and treated as a wife. Disguised as slaves, Nero and his highborn friends prowled the streets of Rome at night, insulting women, and beating and even murdering people at random. One night a senator thus attacked struck Nero. Apparently he then recognized the emperor and apologized. Nevertheless he was ordered to commit suicide. Among Nero's closest friends was Petronius, the author of the *Satyricon,* which gives a vivid picture of the manners of the time. He set the tone of Nero's circle but was the victim of an intrigue by another would-be favorite, Gaius Ofinius Tigellinus, who was one of the two new commanders of the Praetorian Guard appointed after Burrus's death. As a result, Petronius had to kill himself, but he left behind a document that told embarrassing facts about the emperor.

Nero fancied himself an intellectual, liked to pose as a patron of the arts, and had great admiration for the culture of Greece. His poetry, a few lines of which survive, was typical of its time. He wrote an epic poem about the siege of Troy. Among his close companions was the poet Lucan (39–65), nephew of Seneca, who wrote a poem praising Nero. Later they had a falling out, and Lucan joined a conspiracy against Nero and was made to kill himself. Calpurnius (c. 50–60) wrote a poem in which he hailed the handsome and divine young ruler who would bring back a golden age. Nero was also very fond of sculpture, including large statues of himself. He collected and brought to his residences sculptures by such leading Greek artists as Praxiteles.

The young ruler was enthusiastic about chariot racing and other athletic events. He insisted on driving in chariots himself, which was considered a scandalous thing for an emperor to do, but he did not dare do this until after his mother's death. He was so enthusiastic about horses that he had veteran race horses dressed in men's clothing and pensions awarded to them. Nero built a new gymnasium for upper-class youths and a new amphitheater for gladiators to fight in, although, on the grounds that he disliked violent deaths, he decreed that no gladiator should be put to death there. He once had an arena flooded in order to stage a naval battle and he took pleasure in arranging fights among wild beasts. In 60 the emperor established the Neronian games, to be held every five years on the anniversary of his accession to the throne. The games included contests in music and poetry as well as athletics and chariot races. Nero did not participate in the first of these games but nevertheless was declared the winner for oratory.

More than anything, though, Nero wanted to be a singer and actor. At this time the theater was held in low repute by most Romans because it was largely in the hands of Greeks, who were considered inferior. This attitude did not keep Nero from preparing to appear in public, singing to his own accompaniment on the lyre. His first public appearance was at Naples in 64, and no one was allowed to leave the theater while the emperor performed. This resulted in stories of babies being born there and men pretending death in order to be carried out. Nero wrote some of his own songs and he also delighted in appearing in tragic drama. Dio says that "according to report," Nero had "a slight and indistinct voice." In any case, his public appearances as an entertainer scandalized conservative opinion, which found his actions a degrading spectacle for an emperor, but a good deal of the general public was amused.

Along with such activities, Nero found time to dispose in one way or another of a number of people by using the accusation of treason. On his orders, his stepson, Rufius Crispinus, Poppaea's son by another husband, was drowned by the boy's own slaves because he had been playing at being a general and emperor. When Nero thought Rubellius Plautus, also a member of the imperial family, was being talked of as emperor in his place, he ordered him to withdraw to his family's Asian estates. Two years later, in 62, Plautus was ordered to kill himself. Publius Clodius Thrasea Paetus was a senator of uncorruptible principles and a man of republican sympathies. In 66 Nero and his advisers decided that they must be rid of Paetus, so they convicted him of treason. Thrasea Paetus killed himself. By the time Nero had reigned for twelve years, he was the only surviving descendant of the great Augustus.

The most sensational event of Nero's reign was the fire that swept Rome between July 18 and 24, in 64, which resulted in the traditional saying that the emperor "fiddled while Rome burned." Nero was in Anzio when the fire began and returned to Rome when it spread to threaten and then burn his palace. Many public buildings as well as private homes and businesses were destroyed and the loss of life was heavy. Nero threw open undamaged public buildings and gardens to the homeless. He ordered food brought in from the port of Ostia and other nearby towns, and at the same time lowered the price of corn. Many people believed Nero set the fire, one story being that he did so because he wanted to clear land on which to build a new palace. Suetonius says he was guilty of arson but most scholarly opinion is that he did not start the conflagration. As to the story of "fiddling," historians agree that he did take out his lyre and sing a tragic song during the fire, but they don't agree as to where he did his singing.

Nero built a new palace, but he also laid down rules for the rebuilding of the city that were intended to prevent another such fire. Streets were widened and straightened, parts of buildings were ordered to be built of stone, building heights were limited, and owners were required to keep fire-fighting materials handy. The buildings and grounds of *Domus Aurea,* or Golden House, the emperor's new palace, covered 125 acres of the city. The vestibule contained a bronze statue of Nero, 120 feet high, while interior walls were decorated with gold, gems and mother-of-pearl. The main dining room had a ceiling that revolved to keep pace with the sun and the moon, while ivory panels on other dining room ceilings moved to drop flowers on the diners. Pipes sprayed perfume. When the Golden House was ready for the emperor to move in, Nero remarked: "Good, now I can at last begin to live like a human being."

Nero became the first Roman ruler to persecute the comparatively new religious group, the Christians. It is usually assumed that in seeking scapegoats to blame for the fire, he selected the Christians, who were by this time actively propagating their beliefs in Italy, because they were both misunderstood and feared by many Romans. Suetonius called them "a sect professing a new and mischievous religious belief," while Tacitus said they were "hated for their abominable practices." Defenseless and unpopular, the Christians of Rome became victims of Nero's wrath. Some had wild beasts' skins put on them and were left to be torn apart by dogs. Others were set afire after dark in Nero's gardens to provide human torches. According to some accounts, both St. Peter and St. Paul, organizers of the Christian church, met their deaths as part of this persecution after the fire, the former by being crucified head down and the latter by being beheaded. Although they were both martyred about this time, there is no strong evidence that they were indirect victims of the great fire.

Nero's love of everything Greek, not shared by more old-fashioned Romans who admired ancient Greek culture but thought contemporary Greeks were much inferior to themselves, finally led to a long-planned trip to the land of the Hellenes. Nero set out in the fall of 66 with a large entourage and did not return until early 68. Four national festivals of

Greece were held in the same year, which would not usually happen, so that he could participate in all of them. The emperor was awarded every prize even though he did not take part in some contests. In all, during his visit, he won 1,808 prizes. In late November, 67, at the Isthmian games in Corinth, Nero announced that Greece henceforth was "free." In practice this meant immunity from taxes and some measure of self-government, but Greece remained a part of the empire. He also said he would have the Corinth Canal built at once, but only about a fifth of it was completed in his day.

By January, 68, the officials Nero had left in charge of the government in Rome were frantically begging him to return because of plots and threats of revolts against him. Driven by his suspicious mind, his imperial temper and the private and public immorality of the time, in a few years the emperor had created a police state. Secret police increased in numbers and informers were everywhere, while the self-serving men around Nero falsely denounced others to further their own careers. It was no wonder that rumors of plots, if not actual assassination plans, abounded.

One such plot had been discovered in 65 which led to the death of Seneca, among others. A group of conspirators worked out a plan to kill Nero while he attended the Festival of Ceres in April, but a servant of one of the plotters became suspicious of his employer's actions on the eve of the appointed day and told Nero. Gaius Galpurnius Piso, a wealthy, charming and popular figure who enjoyed luxurious living, had been chosen by the plotters to succeed Nero, although he was more a figurehead than an active leader. He killed himself. Eighteen others met death for their part and thirteen more were exiled. Seneca's power was declining at this time, following Burrus's death. Those who disliked him said he was too interested in piling up ever greater wealth, and newer men around Nero were more willing to do the emperor's bidding than was the experienced Seneca. It is doubtful that Seneca had any connection with the Pison conspiracy, but Nero claimed he had and used it as an excuse to order his suicide. Seneca cut his veins and also had poison administered to him. As he slowly died he dictated an essay to his secretaries.

Another conspiracy in 66 resulted in more deaths. The alleged leader of this plot was Annius Vincianus, son-in-law of Corbulo, who had served in the army with him and who may have feared for his own life under Nero. When word of the plot reached Nero in Greece, he summoned Corbulo and two other generals there. As soon as they arrived, without their soldiers who might have protected them, the emperor ordered them to commit suicide. This was the reward Corbulo received for having upheld the emperor's prestige in the contest with Parthia over Armenia.

While he was in Naples in the spring of 68, Nero heard of another plot, this one originating in Gaul (France). Its leader was Gaius Julius Vindex, governor of part of Gaul. He not only issued a proclamation for an uprising against Nero as a tyrant but also called him a second-rate lyre player, which infuriated the emperor. Vindex invited Servius Sulpicius Galba (c. 3 B.C.– A.D. 69), who was then commander of the Roman troops in part of Spain, to become Nero's successor. A Roman army in Germany stayed loyal, however, and defeated Vindex's forces, the latter being killed in the battle. Nero raised a force which he sent off to fight Galba, but the troops showed no enthusiasm for the task. Nero is said meanwhile to have prepared a wild scheme for poisoning all the senators, burning Rome and fleeing to Egypt.

The people of Rome who had enjoyed Nero's exhibitionism for many years turned against him. There was a grain shortage and one story had it that ships were bringing in sand for the site of athletic contests instead of corn and wheat. The commandant of the Praetorian Guard came out in favor of Galba. Nero, hoping eventually to make his way to Egypt, disguised himself in shabby clothing and fled Rome to a nearby villa on the night of June 8, 68. He was frightened on the way by hearing some of the guards denouncing him and also, it is said, by an earthquake. Receiving a message that he had been declared a public enemy, the emperor tried to work up the courage to kill himself, muttering about his cowardice and also at one point, according to Dio, remarking, "Jupiter, what an artist perishes in me." Finally, with the aid of a companion, he thrust a dagger into his throat and died as pursuing troops arrived. Nero's two nurses and his former mistress, Acte, the only persons remaining loyal to him, were permitted to give him a decent burial.

Galba was proclaimed emperor and in October, 68, arrived in Rome. In January, however, troops on the Rhine revolted against him, others joined the uprising and before the end of the month Galba was killed.

The world had not, however, heard the last of Nero. Three different persons claiming to be the emperor appeared and each attracted a following, seeming to indicate that for all his faults some people longed for the spectacles he had once provided. The first false Nero, a slave or a freedman, with the help of some deserters seized an island in the Aegean Sea, but was soon attacked and killed. A man named Terentius Maximus, from Asia Minor, claimed in 79 that he was Nero. He was said to look like the emperor and to play the lyre and sing like him. When he went into Parthian territory King Artabanus was tempted to use him in a quarrel he was then carrying on with the Emperor Titus, but eventually handed him over to the Romans. Finally, in 88, a third impostor appeared. He also fled to Parthia and was also turned over to the Romans.

The most common interpretation of various passages in Revelation, the last book of the Bible, is that they refer to Nero. This book was probably written in its present form when Domitian was emperor, between 81 and 96. Its author was a prophet, exiled on an island in the Aegean, who sought to assure his readers that God, not Satan or the Roman emperor, would prevail in the struggle for the world. The "beast" spoken of in Revelation is said to be Rome and the empire is identified with Nero. The number of the beast is given as 666 and in Hebrew the letters of the name Nero

Caesar have numerical values totaling 666. Not only was Nero feared and hated because he persecuted the Christians, but Revelation also expresses the belief, held in some quarters for hundreds of years, that he is not dead but will return, or that he will rise again. He is seen as the anti-Christ whose second coming will be the evil counterpart of the Second Coming of Jesus Christ, which in those days was expected by Christians to take place in the near future. Even as late as the twelfth century, Pope Paschal II, dreaming that the crows he heard in the trees near the tomb of Nero's family were demons serving the long-dead ruler, had the tomb torn down and a chapel built in its place. Thus did the evil reputation of Nero live on.

Yet Nero was not all bad. He governed well in the early years of his reign, appointing able men to office, and he handled foreign affairs intelligently. He was, at least for a time, conscientious about assuring the Roman people the supply of grain vital to them. His interest in the arts was sincere, even if his own performances were exhibitions of vanity run wild. But Nero was essentially a cowardly man, trapped by his own ancestry and the customs of the time. His inclinations toward intrigue and murder might be said to be hereditary traits, as shown in the acts of his mother, who used the boy in any way that would further her ambitions. His actions were often vicious and cruel and he knew no way to deal with opposition other than to enforce an "off with their heads" policy. Egotistical, extravagant and depraved, Nero was the worst example of the worst aspects of Roman imperial civilization and so has gone down in history as a unique monster.

# Attila: Conqueror Without Roots

Attila the Hun (c. 400–453) was "a man born to shake the races of the world" and "a terror to all lands," according to Priscus, a Greek historian in the service of the East Roman Empire, who met him in A.D. 450 when he was at the height of his power. Fifteen hundred years later, the world still holds this opinion of him.

Attila was also, Priscus wrote, short and squat, with a flat nose, deep-set eyes, a thin gray beard and a swarthy comlex- ion. In these ways, he was physically like his fellow Huns. In later life, his walk was arrogant and his glance insolent, but at the same time he might give audience freely to those who had complaints, handing out rough justice on the spot. Although he was the sole ruler of a fierce people, he never wore a crown and his dress was plain. Even after the loot from raids and wars was plentiful, he spurned dishes of precious metal and ate and drank from wooden utensils. With his family and chieftains, Attila joined in banquets that went on far into the night, with great amounts of alcoholic beverages consumed, but throughout he remained grave and expressionless.

Terrible rages swept Attila at times and his savagery to foes is legendary. A Roman envoy remarked of him that he was a man "driven by some fury," who "seems to strive for the domination of the world." In this drive he almost succeeded. He and his Huns moved over great distances and took Europe by surprise. They conquered many people, seized their cities, slaughtered them by the thousands, and shook the Roman

Empire. Yet the empire Attila founded fell apart almost as soon as he died, the Huns themselves disappeared as a people, and no national state or geographical area remained as a monument to his conquests. The Huns were a rootless people and Attila was a conqueror who put down no roots.

The Huns were one of a number of nomadic peoples who originated somewhere in the vast steppe land of Asia. The steppe, mostly flat grassland with few trees, extends from the lower Danube River in Europe almost all the way across Asia to Manchuria, interrupted here and there by such geographic features as mountains and lakes. Much of this land is unsuitable for agriculture and in many areas the summer season is short. Consequently, the people who inhabited it did not establish villages and cities, or organize their tribal or national life on a geographical basis. They wandered in tribes from place to place with the seasons, seeking pasturage for their livestock, and they often came in contact with each other, a contact that might or might not be peaceful. Sometimes they confronted more settled people who were further advanced in the customs and techniques of civilized societies. Such confrontations resulted from pressure on the nomads to find new sources of food if population growth or a change in the climate left them without enough to eat. In such cases, conflict often resulted, the settled people being forced to protect their property and way of life from the nomads, who had nothing to lose and who were in the habit of fighting for loot, rather than growing food and producing manufactured goods.

Thus for centuries nomadic peoples, mostly of Turkic and Mongol stock, invaded settled and civilized areas, such as China and eastern and western Europe. They often were victorious and either thoroughly looted an area before moving on, or installed themselves as rulers. In some cases the invaders were eventually absorbed by those they conquered, or were replaced as rulers by a fresh wave of nomads not yet softened by agricultural and urban living. A long series of nomadic movements from east to west began with the Scythian

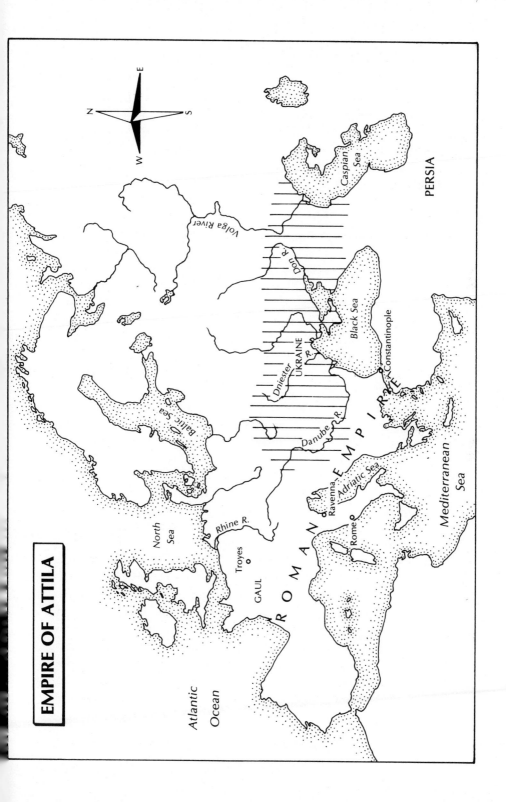

# EMPIRE OF ATTILA

invasion of southern Russia in the eighth century B.C. Two
thousand years later, such invasions reached their climax with
the appearance of the Mongols and their most famous leader,
Jenghiz Khan. The Huns were therefore by no means unique,
but in producing Attila they made certain, without knowing it
at the time, that their name would not disappear from
history's record.

In the eyes of the civilized victims, a nomad was a
"barbarian," a term still used, and properly in this case, to
mean "a rude, wild, uncivilized person" *(Oxford English
Dictionary)*. Even if they had not been so "wild," they were
barbarians to the Europeans, for the Greeks used that term for
anyone not a Greek. The dictionary also notes that barbarian
can mean "one living outside the pale of the Roman Empire
and its civilization," or, even more broadly, "a foreigner, one
whose language and customs differ from the speaker's." The
Huns, therefore, were doubly barbarous.

Scholars disagree as to where and when these particular
barbarians became a recognizable social unit. They may have
been the people the Chinese earlier called the Hsiung-nu,
dwelling north of China at the eastern end of the steppe,
whom the Chinese fought for a long time. The Chinese built
walls, which later became part of the Great Wall, to keep
these marauding barbarians out.

Whatever their origin, the Huns had much in common in
appearance with the Hsiung-nu and with other Asiatic steppe
peoples who thrust themselves upon civilized Asia and Europe
over the centuries. One historian called them "beasts on two
feet" and thought their faces "horrible," but he was a
representative of the races and nations the Huns were
terrorizing. Another wrote: "They have a sort of shapeless
lump, if I may say so, not a face, and pinholes rather than
eyes." The Huns, short and squat, with fat faces, were quite
unlike the racial stock of Europe. They wore loose robes that
were calf-length and split at the sides. Around the waist was a
girdle. Underneath the robe were trousers, gathered at the

ankles, as were the sleeves of the robe at the wrist, as protection against the cold. Short fur capes and fur caps were also part of their regular dress. They wore leather shoes.

The Hun way of life depended primarily on livestock: horses, sheep, cattle and oxen, all of which could provide their own transportation. The sheep were most important, providing not only food but also hides for leather and wool for weaving and felt-making, although there is some doubt that the Huns did much weaving. Hunting provided a good deal of the Huns' food and in some places they may have grown food on a small scale. The nomadic life called for housing that could be put up easily, taken down and transported, so the Huns lived in tents made of felt or sheepskin. After their conquests caused them to take up a more settled existence, as on the Hungarian plains, the nobles lived in timbered houses. Even so, what one writer described as Attila's "palace" consisted of only one room, with a bed screened off at one end by tapestries.

Many goods, such as iron weapons, grain, jewels, gold, silk and wine, were secured by trade, by looting the possessions of defeated enemies, or as tribute (blackmail) paid to keep the Huns from attacking. In trading, the Huns could offer horses, meat, furs and slaves. After they settled near the Danube, trade fairs were held at regular dates along that frontier. At the height of the Huns' power, Attila's nobles ate from silver or gold trays and their bridles were decorated with gold and precious stones. The Huns had a particular craving for gold—they "burned with an infinite thirst for gold," one observer wrote—which they received as tribute in large quantities from the East Roman Empire.

The Huns had little governmental organization above the tribal level until their invasion of Europe required more and better military strategy and leadership. On the steppe they lived in small units—six to ten families dwelling in tents formed a camp, and several of these camps made up a clan. Above this was the tribe, consisting of several clans and numbering about 5,000 people. After they settled down somewhat, a broader organization developed, but still based chiefly on military leadership, with the leaders becoming an aristocratic class.

Prisoners of war became slaves, some of whom served in the army under their masters, some of whom were used for domestic labor. Since they had comparatively little use for slaves in a simple and nomadic economy, the Huns sold many slaves to the Romans. Women were accorded considerable respect and were not held in seclusion, although because of the nature of the Huns' way of life they labored hard. A man could have several wives if he could afford them. Roman observers considered the Huns cruel to their children because of a custom of cutting the cheeks of male babies the day they were born so that they would learn to endure pain before they received milk.

The Huns practiced a pagan religion and looked to shamans, who, like medicine men elsewhere, were magicians, healers and seers. The shaman could communicate with the spirits that dwelled in nature. Future events were predicted by reading the signs to be seen in the entrails of animals and in the streaks on their bones. Various attempts to convert the Huns to Christianity were made but with little success.

Only in warfare were the Huns superior to the nations with whom they came in contact. Their chief weapon was the bow and arrow, although they also carried swords, lances and lassos or nets, which they used to entrap an enemy. As cavalrymen they were skilled marksmen with great maneuverability. Charging swiftly and fiercely, they might as quickly swerve, retreat and regroup to charge from another direction before the foe could prepare to meet the new attack. When they were forced on the defensive, they formed their wagons into a rough circle, as the American pioneers on the western plains did centuries later.

It was the close relationship of the Hun warrior and his horse that marked him off from other soldiers. "They spend their lives on horseback," a Roman historian declared, "sometimes astride, sometimes sideways, like women. They hold

their meetings thus; they buy and sell, drink and eat—even
sleep, lying on the necks of their mounts. In battle they swoop
upon the enemy, uttering frightful yells." The Hun horse was
not a large, handsome creature but a smaller, sturdy animal,
hardened to cold. Some observers claimed that Hun warriors
put raw meat under the saddles of their horses to warm it and
ate it while riding. Actually, they used raw meat this way to
prevent or heal wounds caused by the pressure of the saddle
on the horse. Observers were right, though, when they
reported that these "horrible" men, who seemed riveted to
their horses, struck terror into the Europeans who faced them
in battle.

It remains to be said of the Huns as a people and to point
out its implications, that they were illiterate and left no
written records. In addition, because of their nomadic life and
because they secured most if not all of their metal weapons
and other goods by trade or looting, they left no archeological
remains. They did not even mint their own coins, which can
often tell quite a bit about a nation and a people. What we
know of them today is based on the writings of some Greek
and Roman travelers and historians, all of whom abhorred the
Huns and thought them cruel and savage with no redeeming
traits. The historical record is therefore very much biased,
even though it is the product of writers whose own civilizations practiced slavery, put on gladiatorial combats, and
punished criminals by crucifixion.

Amianus Marcellinus (c. 330–95), a Greek, was one of these
historians. He hated all barbarians, especially the Huns, but
probably never laid eyes on a Hun, so he had to rely on others
for his information. Priscus, already quoted, had the advantage
of firsthand contact with the Huns, but had the same natural
prejudices as other Greeks and Romans. His writings have
survived only in fragments. Sidonius Apollinaris (c. 430–c.
479), who was born in Gaul of a noble family and became a
bishop, saw the Huns as did others: noses "a shapeless, flat
excrescence" and eyes whose "piercing gaze commands the
farthest expanses." Lastly, there is Jordanes, who lived in the

sixth century, long after Attila died. Probably a Goth, Jordanes became a priest and wrote a history of the Ostrogoths, which involved the Huns. These authors were not, for the most part, writing about the Huns as such but about the Roman Empire. They considered the Huns only as their actions affected the empire.

The Huns these writers feared so much appeared in Europe about the year 370 when, after having swept across Asia, they invaded the lower Volga River valley, north of the Caspian Sea. What force propelled them from the Asiatic steppes into Europe is not known. Quite likely it was a search for more plentiful food supplies and they were rewarded when they pushed on westward into the Ukraine, in what is now southwestern European Russia.

Here the Ostrogoths, seemingly secure in a prosperous empire they founded in the Ukraine, were suddenly confronted by the roving Huns. The Goths, a Germanic people, left their original homeland in southern Scandinavia about the beginning of the Christian era. By the year 238 they were far enough south to raid the Roman Empire, as the Huns were to do two centuries later. One branch, the Ostrogoths, settled in an area north of the Black Sea and carved out an empire that extended from the Dniester River, which runs into the Black Sea, on the west, eastward to the Don River and the headwaters of the Volga. The Huns swept into this rich agricultural land and by 375 conquered it. In that year the Ostrogoths' aging and discouraged king, Ermanaric, killed himself as the Huns overran his kingdom. He was succeeded by his great-nephew Vithimiris, who within a year was killed in one of a number of losing battles against the Huns.

Many Ostrogoths fled westward, pursued by the Huns. This movement brought both into the territory of the Visigoths who had established a nation west of the Dniester River. Fording that river in the rear of the army of Athanaric, the Visigoth chief, the Huns fell on the Goths and scattered them. Athanaric then tried to establish a line of defense nearer the Danube, farther west. Again the Huns surprised their foe but were unable to complete their victory because by now they were too encumbered by booty to maneuver in their usual swift style. Athanaric fled, first to Transylvania and then to Constantinople, where he died in 381.

By the fall of 376 the pressure of the Huns drove as many as 200,000 Goths to seek safety by crossing the Danube River and entering the territory of the Roman Empire. They were so anxious to escape the horde that was "sweeping away and destroying everything that came its way," and so threatened by famine, that they were prepared to force their way into Roman territory. They were given permission to cross the Danube after which they became an unsettling influence within the empire, eventually sacking Rome in 410 under the leadership of Alaric I.

In the late fourth century the Roman Empire still ruled most of Europe, North Africa and a good deal of the Middle East, but it was by no means immune to hostile forces both from within and without. From this time into the sixth century, the empire was attacked not only by Huns and Goths, but also by Avars, Teutons and Slavs. The empire split into two parts after the death of Emperor Theodosius the Great in 395. One of his sons, Honorius, became emperor of the West and ruled from 395 to 423, first from Rome and then, after 402, from Ravenna, a city in northeastern Italy near the Adriatic Sea. Another son, Arcadius, became ruler of the East Roman, or Byzantine, Empire, from 395 to 408. His capital was Constantinople (formerly Byzantium and now Istanbul, on the Bosporus in northwestern Turkey).

The East Empire was the wealthier and stronger of the two and so was in a better position than the West Empire to deal with the Huns, either by paying tribute or by fighting them. As the two empires more and more went their own ways, the rulers in the east did their best to divert the Huns westward and they seldom helped their brother rulers in Rome and Ravenna. The Huns thus could play off the two governments against each other.

In the east, the emperors who faced the menace of the Huns

were Theodosius II (401–50) and Marcian (386–457). Theodosius, who preferred to study theology and astronomy, became emperor in 408, with his sister, Pulcheria (399–453), as co-ruler. In 421, he married Eudocia (d. 460), a Greek, and came under the influence of both women. Marcian succeeded Theodosius in 450 and married Pulcheria. He took a firmer stand against the Huns.

In the west, Valentinian III (419–55) became emperor in 425, two years after his uncle Honorius died, when Theodosius of the East Empire deposed a usurper who had sat on the western imperial throne for two years. Valentinian was a lazy and ineffective ruler.

The Huns' first direct assault on the territory and armies of the Roman Empire began in 395 when a force of the barbarians crossed the Don River near its mouth and rode south through the Caucasus into Persia and the Roman provinces south and southwest of Armenia. Apparently driven by a serious food shortage, the Huns seized food, livestock and many prisoners. When they got as far west as the Euphrates River, however, the Romans attacked them and destroyed at least one group. In 397 the Huns again broke into these Roman lands but were driven out.

In these raids the Huns as usual horrified their enemies. St. Jerome (c. 347–420?), the scholar and early leader of the Christian church, who lived in the Middle East after 386, left a vivid account: "They filled the whole earth with slaughter and panic alike as they flitted hither and thither on their swift horses. . . . by their speed they outstripped rumor, and they took pity neither upon religion nor rank nor age nor wailing childhood."

The reader may wonder why, with the exception of Attila, no individual Hun has been named as yet, while a number of Romans, Greeks and Goths have been discussed. There are two reasons, the first being the point noted earlier that the Huns were unable to keep their own written record. In the second place, the Huns for a long time had no large-scale or permanent governmental organization. Groups formed temporarily under leaders for travel or for raiding purposes, and only later as they became more settled and faced well-organized enemies did formal leaders of larger groups of Huns emerge.

The first such leader known by name was Uldis, who attacked the Goths in Rumania in 400 and who might be called a king of the Huns but not of all of them. In 404–5 he led a force into the Balkan Peninsula provinces of the empire and invaded Thrace at the southeastern end of the peninsula. In 408 he crossed the Danube and captured a fortress. But, as was true of most barbarian groups, Uldis and his Huns also at times assisted both the East and West Roman Empires in fighting off other enemies. In 400, for example, Uldis fought the Germans under their leader Gainas and for this the East Roman Empire gave him handsome gifts and concluded a treaty. It was common by this time for barbarians to serve as mercenaries in the Roman armies. Uldis was defeated in 408 and disappears from history.

By the late 420's, another name appears as that of the chief military leader of the Huns. This was Rua, who shared his power with a brother, Octar, and perhaps with another brother, Mundiuch. Rua felt himself strong enough in 434 to demand from the Romans in Constantinople that they return to him some subject people who had fled from his domain. He threatened war if his demand was not met but he died just as the campaigning season of 434 arrived. Rua was succeeded by two sons of Mundiuch, Bleda and Attila. Bleda was the elder and a rough, boisterous man. Not much is known about him, except that he took a great fancy to a Moorish dwarf named Zerco and was continually and vastly amused by the unfortunate man's stammering speech and ungainly walk, while Attila was unable to stand the sight of Zerco. Bleda ruled over the tribes in the east and Attila over those in the west, but the brothers did not get along. Each was eager for power and the struggle ended in 445 when Attila murdered Bleda.

Attila took advantage of the naive beliefs of his followers to further establish his rule. A Hun herdsman, one of whose heifers cut its foot on something buried in the ground, discovered the object to be an old sword and took it to Attila. Attila declared it was the ancient sword of the war god and that its delivery to him meant that he was to be acknowledged supreme ruler and that he was assured of becoming the conqueror of the world.

Before Bleda's murder, the brothers had continued Rua's demands on the East Romans. They conferred with Roman envoys in 435 at the city of Margus on the Danube and demanded, among other things, that no more fugitives be allowed to escape into the empire from the Huns' dominions. Moreover, they convinced the Romans that it was to their advantage to double the yearly tribute of gold to the Huns to 700 pounds. All through these negotiations, the Huns insisted on remaining mounted on their horses. The Romans, not wishing to have to stand and look up to the Huns, were forced to do the same, to their apparent discomfort.

Two years later, Attila and Bleda were induced by the West Roman commander, Aetius, who was already well known to them, to attack the Burgundians. These German people, who had indirectly been driven across the Rhine River by the Huns' westward expansion, settled in 413 on the middle Rhine. They caused the Romans trouble in 435 by invading Upper Belgica, an area around the cities of Trier and Metz, so Aetius was eager to crush them. This the Huns did for him, killing, according to one account, 20,000 Burgundians, including their king, Gundahar.

The year 441 saw the Huns attacking East Roman territory on the grounds that the treaty made at Margus in 435 was being violated. They claimed that the bishop of Margus had crossed the Danube and robbed the graves of some royal Huns, stealing treasure which had been buried with them. They also alleged that the Romans had not, as promised, returned some fugitives to them. The Romans denied both charges, but the Huns seem to have been right. Under Bleda and Attila, they crossed the Danube and destroyed a number of towns, including the important city of Viminacium. Some of the people of Margus wanted the bishop turned over to the Huns to prevent further slaughter. The bishop, in turn, suspecting that this would happen, offered to betray the city to the Huns. Attila agreed. One night the bishop had the gates opened, and the Huns swarmed in and devastated Margus so completely that it was never rebuilt. The Huns went on to raze more cities, including Singidunum (now Belgrade, Yugoslavia).

A truce was concluded but two years later the Emperor Theodosius, with less pressure on his military forces in other parts of the empire, dared to refuse to turn over any fugitives. This refusal so angered Attila that he unleashed his Huns in a savage campaign of destruction. The city of Ratiaria, base of the empire's Danube fleet, was destroyed and its residents enslaved. Riding on, the Huns captured and completely destroyed the city of Nish, in what is now eastern Yugoslavia. The next city to fall was Sardica (now Sofia, the capital of Bulgaria) and its fall left open the way to the imperial city of Constantinople.

On this move south, Attila came up against the East Roman army, which he defeated in several battles. The Huns pushed on to the Black Sea north of Constantinople and the Sea of Marmara south of it, but this kind of fast-moving cavalry was not equipped to besiege what was probably the most strongly defended city in the world. Meanwhile, one Hun squadron, encumbered as usual by booty and captives, was defeated, but a final battle utterly routed the last Roman force and Theodosius had no choice but to admit defeat. Attila's terms were harsh. The fugitives were given over to him at once, 6,000 pounds of gold were paid as arrears from other years, and thereafter Attila would receive 2,100 pounds a year, three times the previous annual tribute.

Such tributes, when expressed in pounds of gold, sound like tremendous sums, but were well within the means of the Byzantine Empire. In the fifth century the empire's revenue from taxes and other sources amounted to about 270,000 pounds of gold a year, while the Empress Eudocia at one time gave 200 pounds just to restore the public baths at Antioch.

The Huns also received gold for troops they furnished to the empire and were paid in gold for each prisoner of war they returned. Much of this precious metal found its way back to the Romans, for the Huns needed the goods which Roman manufacturers and traders could supply.

By the mid-440's the Huns were beginning to settle down in the lands they had conquered, but they still practiced pillaging as their chief occupation. They again invaded the East Roman Empire in 448, apparently without any excuse. Attila planned an attack on an even larger scale than before and included in his forces men from subject races such as the Gepids and the Goths. In Thrace the Huns met the Roman army, commanded by a German, Arnegisclus, and in a hotly contested battle defeated him. For once, though, the Huns suffered such heavy casualties that their military power was weakened. Nevertheless, they proceeded to lay waste the Balkan provinces, destroying many cities and, in the words of the author of a biography of St. Hypatius: "There were so many murders and blood-letting that the dead could not be numbered. Ay, for they took captive the churches and monasteries and slew the monks and maidens in great numbers." Peace came in 448, but this time Attila demanded and received a large territory south of the Danube, about 300 miles long and 100 or more miles wide, which the Romans were to evacuate entirely. With this land gone, as well as fortifications and cities along the Danube, that river no longer was a defensible boundary of the Roman Empire.

One of Attila's most important lieutenants, Edeco, was sent to Constantinople in the spring of 449 to complain to the imperial court that the treaty of the previous years was not being observed by the Romans. At court a eunuch named Chrysaphius, the emperor's most powerful minister, offered a large reward if Edeco would murder Attila when he returned. Edeco agreed—or pretended to agree—and a mission was organized to visit Attila, on the pretext of delivering an answer to his complaint about the treaty. The embassy was headed by Maximinus, a distinguished official of the empire, who did not know of the plot. Fortunately, in view of what it added to our knowledge of Attila and the Huns, Maximinus invited the historian Priscus to accompany him.

The expedition left Constantinople in the early summer of 449 and crossed the Danube near where Attila lived, after many days' journey. Before much could be accomplished, Attila and his court moved on to another village, but apparently Edeco had already told his king of the assassination plot. Amid threats and arguments, a discussion between the Huns and the Romans continued off and on for months, resulting in another peace treaty that was favorable to the empire by the early summer of 450. In late July, however, Emperor Theodosius died as a result of a fall from his horse and was succeeded by Marcian, who refused to pay further tribute.

The most interesting result of the embassy of 449, so far as later ages are concerned, was the firsthand account Priscus composed. He relates, for example, that when Attila entered the village where negotiations were held, maidens came to meet him, "advancing before him in rows under fine white linen cloths stretched out to such a length that under each cloth, which was held up by the hands of women along either side, seven or even more girls walked." When Attila came to the house of his chief lieutenant, Onegesius, the latter's wife and servants came out with wine and food to offer the king, who ate and drank sitting on his horse.

Some days later, the Romans were invited to a banquet. Attila sat in the middle on a couch, and with wine in an ivy-wood cup saluted his guests in order of rank, while each of them returned the salutation. "While sumptuous food had been prepared—served on silver plates—for the other barbarians and us," Priscus continued, "for Attila there was nothing but meat on a wooden trencher. He showed himself temperate in all other ways too. . . . His dress, too, was plain, having care for nothing other than to be clean." After the feast, two barbarians sang, chanting songs of tribute to Attila. The king remained unmoved, "except when his youngest son . . . came in and stood before him. He pinched the lad's cheeks and looked on him with serene eyes."

Priscus visited Hereca, Attila's chief wife, noting that the houses in the area where she lived were made of "carved planks beautifully fitted together, and others of clean beams smoothly planed straight; they were laid on timbers which formed circles." He found Hereca "lying on a soft spread. The floor was covered with mats of felted wool. A number of servants were waiting on her in a circle, and maid-servants, sitting on the floor in front of her, were embroidering with colors fine linens to be placed as ornament over their barbarian clothes."

A curious incident in Attila's life, which involved Honoria, the sister of the Emperor Valentinian III, occurred in 450. Honoria, who had more intelligence and energy than her brother, was charged with having an affair with her steward. To escape a forced marriage to a rich and respectable Roman senator, Herculanus, she sent a eunuch named Hyacinth to Attila, begging him to rescue her. She also sent her ring, the implication being that she wanted Attila to marry her. Word of her plot leaked out and she was placed in the custody of her mother, Placidia. Attila claimed Honoria as his wife and warned the West Roman government not to harm her because, he asserted, as her husband he should receive her inheritance of half the western empire. Valentinian's officials pointed that half the empire did not belong to her because all inheritance was through the male line. So the matter ended. In the light of history, it is probable that Honoria was trying to depose Valentinian and become empress, while Attila could use the rebuff he received as an excuse to attack the empire.

Toward the end of the year 450, Attila was faced with the problem of whom to attack next. He had been planning to assault the West Empire but the accession of Marcian to the throne in Constantinople caused him to consider war in that area because the new emperor took such a firm stand against paying tribute. Attila finally decided to invade the west and in early 451 he led his army westward from the Hungarian plains, intending to attack the Visigoths. Contemporary accounts say his army numbered half a million men, but this is probably an exaggeration. In any event, he crossed the Rhine on April 7, 451, and captured the city of Metz. Advancing into Gaul, the Roman province corresponding roughly to present-day France, he besieged Orleans, southwest of Paris, but was repulsed. He then withdrew eastward toward Troyes.

The army opposing Attila consisted partly of Roman troops, with a large contingent of Visigoths. It was commanded by the very capable Flavius Aetius (c. 396–454), who, under Valentinian III, was in reality the effective ruler of the western empire. Aetius was well known to the Huns and, in fact, had been friendly with their leaders. Defeated by a rival, Aetius had taken refuge with the Huns in 432, when Rua was their chief, and twenty years before that he had been left as a hostage with the Huns to insure the carrying out of a treaty. Aetius later conferred on Attila the title of Master of the Soldiers of the West Empire, although this did not involve actually commanding Roman troops. It did, however, give the holder substantial pay and grain for his own soldiers.

The two most successful military commanders of the time faced each other in a showdown battle which took place near Troyes, about June 20, 451. The Goths, under their elderly King Theodoric, held the right flank of the Roman line while Aetius's troops were on the left, with some Alans of dubious loyalty in the center. Attila and the Huns led the center of their forces with subject troops on either flank. The battle began with the Huns losing a hill they had occupied earlier but they then pierced the center of the Roman battle line and threw their strength against the Visigoths, whose king was killed in the struggle. The Goths rallied and charged on the Huns' flanks forcing Attila to retreat into the usual protection of his circle of wagons as night came. Jordanes in his history says that 165,000 men were killed but this seems far too large a figure. Attila was in danger of being completely overwhelmed, but Aetius, wanting the Huns available in the future as a counterforce against other barbarians, allowed them to retreat from Gaul without further fighting. If the Huns had won a clear-cut victory at Troyes, most if not all of Western Europe would probably have been under their domination for some time.

Despite this setback, Attila prepared for a campaign in 452 but once again postponed his threatened attack on Marcian and the East Roman Empire. He decided to invade Italy and assault the heart of the West Roman Empire directly, partly in revenge for the previous year's defeat. With another large army, Attila crossed the Julian Alps into northeastern Italy and began his usual course of destruction. The city of Aquileia put up such a strong defense that Attila had to send for some of his subject peoples, or perhaps Roman prisoners, who knew how to build and operate siege engines. When the city fell, it was plundered and razed to the ground and its citizens were massacred. The Huns swept on, taking other cities, including Verona and Milan, although for some unknown reason they did not plunder the latter in their usual manner.

The Romans were helpless and had no choice but to negotiate with Attila. Aetius asked for peace and a delegation met with Attila. The delegation was headed by Pope Leo I (c. 400–461), who was pope from 440 until his death and who to later generations became known as St. Leo the Great. He was an outstanding figure of his age and through his efforts the authority of the pope in Rome over all other Christian bishops was confirmed. Although he sometimes has been given credit for the Huns' withdrawal from Italy, the real reasons were otherwise. Near famine conditions existed at this time and disease was breaking out. Attila's army was weakened by its campaign, even though successful in some ways, and an East Roman force had defeated the Hun army left to protect the home territories. Once again Attila had spread devastation and terror but had accomplished nothing of a lasting nature.

Knowing no other way of life than to plunder neighbors and enemies, Attila prepared to attack the East Roman Empire in 453. First, though, he decided early in the year to take another wife, a young woman named Ildico, probably of Germanic origin and said to be beautiful. After celebrating far into the night of their marriage, Attila and his bride retired. When the king did not appear by late the next day, his attendants entered his quarters. They found that their leader had bled to death through the nose in his sleep. The man who had terrified Europe was gone at the age of fifty-three, or possibly a few years more.

The Huns cut off their hair and slashed themselves with swords to show their grief. Attila's body was placed in a tent of silk while skilled horsemen rode rapidly around it to gladden the heart of the dead. After a song was sung over the body, Attila was placed in a grave. The coffin was bound with iron to show he was a conqueror and gold and silver to attest to the tribute paid him by two empires. Those in charge of the ceremony then killed the men who dug the grave so that it would not be discovered and despoiled.

Attila's sons (just how many of them there were is not clear) divided the empire on the basis of groups of Huns and subject people rather than land. In a matter of months the brothers were fighting each other. In a few more months, many of the subject people, especially the Gepids and the Ostrogoths, revolted and in a battle in 454 on the Nedao River in Pannonia, a province southwest of the Danube, they defeated the quarreling heirs of Attila, killing the eldest, Ellac. The Huns withdrew toward the Black Sea from where they had first startled Europe. The short-lived Hun Empire was dead.

The Huns under Attila and earlier leaders accomplished nothing except to raise their own standard of living somewhat by plundering other people and exacting tribute. Even this was done at the cost of the lives of thousands of Hun soldiers, but that was a fate more or less expected in that era. They contributed nothing to the arts or to science and technology, or to the governing of nations. They caused havoc in many parts of the Roman dominions, and thereby weakened the empire. On the other hand, by defeating other barbarians, especially the Germanic peoples, they helped keep such groups from breaking up the Roman Empire.

Attila's only legacy to the modern world, in fact, was to give his name, and that of his people, as synonyms for frightfulness. Under the name of Etzel, Attila appears as king in the Germanic myth of the Nibelungen, an evil family that owns a hoard of gold which is magic in nature and bears a curse. An epic of the early thirteenth century tells a complicated and bloody tale of events at the court of Etzel, who, in the end, is one of the few survivors. Between 1853 and 1874 Richard Wagner, the German composer, wrote a cycle of four operas, *Der Ring des Nibelungen*, based in part on this epic and hence in part on Attila.

In Christian legend, Attila became the "Scourge of God," or *Flagellum Dei* in Latin writings, who brought divine vengeance on the world. If it was not a flattering way to go down in history, it was at least an evalution of the terrorizing force of his personality and his deeds.

# Jenghiz Khan: Conquest for Conquest's Sake

Jenghiz Khan (c. 1167–1227), with his ferocious Mongol warriors, founded a dynasty that in one century conquered a larger empire than the Romans did in four. Many who experienced this upheaval felt, however, as did an Islamic observer: "It is unlikely that mankind will see the like of this calamity until the world comes to an end and perishes."

The great khan's beginnings were humble enough. His father, Yesugei, was born about 1140, the chief of a small sub-clan at a time when Mongol power was at a low point. His mother, Hoelun, became the bride of Yesugei when he and two of his brothers seized her as she traveled home with a young Mongol she had just wed. She bore Yesugei five children, of whom Jenghiz Khan was the oldest. When he was born, beside the Onon River in Mongolia, he was clutching a clot of blood in his fist and this was thought to be an omen that he would become a great hero when he grew up. He was called Temujin, after a Tatar chief his father had recently captured, it being customary to name a child for some auspicious event. Temujin grew to be tall and sturdy, with a broad forehead and "cat's eyes." The hard life he led hardened him to wounds and cold and helped develop his iron will.

The origins of the Mongols are obscure but they are closely related to other peoples of the steppe lands of northeast Asia, such as the Huns. Before Jenghiz Khan unified them, the Mongols were loosely confederated but fought regularly among themselves. They lived in what is now the Mongolian

People's Republic, between the Onon and Kerulen rivers, migrating with the seasons to feed their livestock. The typical Mongol had a broad face, flat nose, prominent cheekbones, eyes that seemed to be slits, and straight black hair. They were mostly short and stocky.

The Mongols' way of life was much like that of Attila's Huns in earlier days. They were organized in clans, and sometimes in sub-clans, based on blood relationships. Several clans would often confederate to form a larger tribal unit. Their homes were circular, made of wood frames and covered with skins, and could be transported easily on their black-painted wagons. They lived mostly on milk and meat from their herds and flocks and from game taken in hunting. The horse of the Mongol was small but sturdy and with its rider made a military unit that was fast and able to endure extreme hardships. Men dominated this rude society and could have a number of wives. The women drove the wagons and put up and took down the tent houses.

Until the time of Jenghiz Khan, the Mongols kept no written records, but after his death one of his sons ordered the compilation, in 1240, of what became known as *The Secret History of the Mongols*. It is the primary source of knowledge today about the khan and his conquests. Two Christian travelers and one Moslem, writing after the khan's death, also provide useful and interesting information about the Mongols and their empire. Giovanni Carpini (c. 1180–1252), a Franciscan monk, was sent by the pope in 1245 to visit the Mongols at the city of Karakorum in Mongolia. After his return in 1247 he wrote the first account to appear in Europe. Juvaini (1226–1283), a member of a distinguished Moslem family, also went to Karakorum as a young man and while there began to write his *History of the World Conqueror*. Somewhat later the famous traveler Marco Polo (1254?–1324) composed the story of his travels, which includes some acute observations about the Mongols of the late thirteenth century.

When Temujin was about nine years old, his father set out to find a bride for him and did so at the camp of another chief

of a small clan. The girl's name was Borte. Yesugei left Temujin with his future bride's family, and warned them that the boy was afraid of dogs. On his way home, Yesugei met some Tatars, another and generally unfriendly ethnic group of the steppes, who invited him to eat with them. He did so and was given a slow-acting poison that killed him soon after he reached home. Yesugei's few followers abandoned his widow, Hoelun, and her children, including Temujin, who returned home to help support the family by hunting and fishing. During this trying period, Temujin and his brother quarreled with two half-brothers, accusing the latter of appropriating fish and game they had caught. The dispute was settled one day when the two boys shot and killed one of the half-brothers, Bekter, with their arrows.

The chief of a Taijiut tribe, anxious that no successor to Yesugei arise to be his overlord, determined to capture Temujin and succeeded in doing so after the boy, then about 15, evaded his pursuers for nine days. As a prisoner, he wore a *cangue* around his neck, a wooden frame several feet square that acted like a portable pillory. Despite this, he managed to escape and rejoin his family. The small family group remained on the verge of starvation and appeared doomed when raiders made off with eight of the nine horses they owned. On the steppes only horses gave mobility—the vital ability to move from place to place in search of food. Temujin set out alone on the remaining horse and after several days caught up with the raiders. With the aid of a young man named Bo'orchu, whom he met and who joined him in the pursuit, he daringly took back his horses and escaped. Bo'orchu remained a lifelong friend and became one of the khan's highest-ranking commanders.

Temujin, when about seventeen, went to claim his bride, Borte, and the ceremony was celebrated. As the bride's dowry, her family presented Temujin and his mother with a luxurious black sable cloak. Although later as khan Temujin took several other wives, Borte remained the one he relied on for support and advice. She also bore him sons, a very important matter in

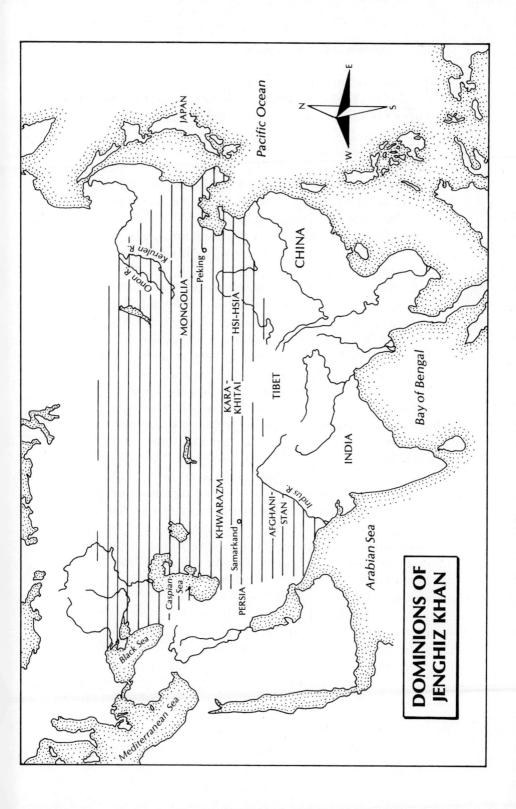

DOMINIONS OF
JENGHIZ KHAN

that tribal society. They were, in order, Jochi, Jagatai, Ogodai and Tolui. Temujin, intent on building up the size and strength of his clan, did not enjoy the company of his young wife for long. A large group of Merkit warriors, another Mongol tribe that had long been enemies of the group Temujin belonged to, staged a surprise raid. Temujin, the other men and the horses escaped, but Borte was left behind as there was not enough transportation. She was seized and taken away by the Merkits and given to one of their chiefs. The story makes Temujin sound unchivalrous by later standards, but at that time preservation of fighting strength was all-important; women were easily available.

Even so, Temujin did not intend to suffer this insult and loss for long. He made his way to the camp of Togrul, chief of the Keraits, a strong tribe that controlled the land west of the Mongols. Temujin's father had at one time aided Togrul in battle and had become his blood brother, or *anda*. Taking the sable cloak as a gift, Temujin begged Togrul to help him and the latter agreed. Also involved was Jamuqa, about Temujin's age but head of a stronger clan of Mongols. The two had met as boys and had played together and each considered himself the other's *anda*. Togrul and Jamuqa are said to have assembled between them 40,000 horsemen. This force fell on the Merkit camp where Borte was being held and by good luck Temujin came upon her in the confusion surrounding the raid. He at once sent word to Togrul and Jamuqa: "She whom I sought, she whom I grieved for, I have found."

The friendship between Temujin and Jamuqa broke down in a year or two because of their rivalry to restore the old Mongol monarchy, each wanting to be the new khan. At the crucial point, it was Borte's advice that caused Temujin to decide to break with his *anda*. Most of the other important leaders threw their support to Temujin and about 1196 they chose him as khan, or king of the Mongols. Through his own efforts the young man had risen from poverty and a complete lack of power to become one of the rulers of the Mongolian steppes by the time he was thirty years old. A few years later, probably in 1201, other chiefs who would not accept Temujin elected Jamuqa as a rival khan. Temujin and Jamuqa each had about 30,000 followers and they fought each other several times. On one occasion Jamuqa fell on a clan allied with Temujin, defeated it and had its seventy leading men boiled alive. Such an action was considered needlessly cruel even for those times and helped drive other tribes into Temujin's camp. Unlike Jamuqa, he treated his allies with respect and showed better judgment in organizing his followers.

In one engagement between the forces of the two rivals, the battle of Koyitan, a raging storm dispersed Jamuqa's army but not Temujin's. Temujin and his followers saw this as a sign that the gods favored them. Jamuqa's allies scattered and he, turning against them, pillaged some of their camps. In another fight, the battle of Khalakhaljit, Temujin's forces were outnumbered and while the result was a standoff, he was forced to order a retreat. As a result, some of his allies deserted him temporarily. The bitter rivalry for rule of the Mongols ended finally in 1205 in the bloody battle of Chakirma'ut. Jamuqa's forces suffered heavy casualties and others deserted so that in the end only five companions remained. These men seized him and took him to the khan where Jamuqa asked to be put to death. Temujin had this done but in what was considered the most respectful way. Jamuqa was rolled up in a carpet and crushed to death. It was believed that a man's spirit was in his blood and so by killing him without shedding blood the spirit was preserved.

In these years the contest for power with Jamuqa was not the only matter that occupied Jenghiz Khan in his drive for ever wider rule. His ally Togrul was deposed by his brother, with the aid of the Naiman tribe. Togrul went to the khan, who led his warriors against Togrul's brother and restored Togrul to his throne. The two then joined to defeat the Merkit. To show his devotion to Togrul, who had been like a foster father, Temujin allowed him to keep all the booty secured from pillaging the Merkits.

The Chinese empire, with its capital in Peking, encouraged

Jenghiz Khan and Togrul to join them in fighting the Tatars, who were harassing the northern Chinese border lands. The Tatars were a Turkic tribe in Mongolia, speaking a language different from the Mongols'. Later they were absorbed into other groups but Europeans came to call all the barbarian invaders from Asia by the name of Tatar. The first campaign against the Tatars, in 1198, was a success as far as booty was concerned and the Mongols and the Keraits profited greatly. In addition, the Chinese empire conferred titles on both Togrul and Temujin, making the former a "wang," or prince, and giving the latter a lesser title. The Chinese title provided Temujim with additional prestige among the people of the steppes, although it also indicated that at this time Togrul was considered the more important chief. In defeating the Tatars, Temujin avenged the death of his father and now controlled all of eastern Mongolia.

The khan decided on a final campaign of elimination against the Tatars in 1202 and in a hard-fought battle completely crushed them. Many prisoners were taken, and while some were kept as slaves, Temujin declared: "We will exterminate every male standing higher than a wagon axle." He also showed on this occasion that he would accept no disobedience to his orders, one of which was that no one was to stop to collect booty until the battle was won, when all would share. Three Mongol princes disobeyed the khan on this occasion and they were punished by having all their loot taken away.

While he was increasing his power during this period, Jenghiz Khan added three more wives and acquired two followers who became trusted generals. After the defeat of the Tatars, Temujin took as part of his share of booty the daughter of a Tatar chief, named Yisugen. The young woman seems not only to have welcomed this event but she also told the khan that she had a beautiful older sister. The khan thereupon wed Yisui, too. In 1204 a Merkit chief, wishing to acknowledge final submission to the khan, offered him his daughter, Qulan, and Temujin married her, although not without some worry about his first wife's reaction. Borte offered no objections and

Qulan became one of the khan's favorite wives and was celebrated in Mongol poetry for her beauty.

In the battle of Koyitan against Jamuqa, Jenghiz Khan's horse had been wounded by an arrow. A captured enemy soldier later admitted to having done the deed but promised that if he were spared punishment he would "go at your behest to attack all your enemies." Much taken by the soldier's bold confession, the khan spared him and renamed him Jebe, "The Arrow." He became a notable commander, defeating Persians and Russians, among others, for the khan. In a battle with the Taijiuts, Temujin was wounded in the neck by an arrow. He kept on fighting but by nightfall collapsed exhausted. A loyal follower from another tribe stayed with him and sucked the blood from the wound to prevent infection. The young man, Jelmei, became one of the khan's four best generals.

Temujin and Togrul, the wang khan, joined forces again in 1202 to launch an expedition against the Naimans, a powerful tribe of western Mongolia. After defeating one Naiman army, they met with another while returning to their own lands. Since it was late in the day, both sides prepared to fight a battle the following morning. During the night, however, Togrul, perhaps fearing that Temujin, who technically was still his vassal, was becoming too powerful, ordered his army to decamp. He left his fires lighted as though his men were still there. In the morning when Temujin found himself deserted, he had no choice but to retreat, which he did in an orderly manner. Not long after, Togrul, while withdrawing, met defeat at the hands of still more Naimans. His recent treachery did not keep him from begging Temujin for aid and the latter sent the help which rescued Togrul from disaster.

Relations between the two and their people continued to deteriorate. Jenghiz Khan was badly insulted when Togrul refused to give his daughter in marriage to one of his sons. War broke out and in the first encounter Temujin's forces were badly beaten. Some of his followers forsook him and he was forced to retreat to the extreme northern part of Mongol territory. By the fall of 1203, however, he had with his usual burning energy reorganized his forces and returned to the war. After a secret march, he surprised the Keraits and broke up their army in the battle of Mount Jeje'er. Togrul fled to the west into Naiman territory where a Naiman officer, not recognizing him, killed him. The Keraits submitted to Jenghiz Khan and served him loyally thereafter.

With the defeat and death of both Togrul and Jamuqa, and after a final victory over the Naimans, the once-hunted boy Temujin was now, when still not forty years old, supreme throughout Mongolia, over all Turkic and Mongol people. His power extended about 1,000 miles east and west and 600 miles from north to south. To confirm his position, Temujin summoned leaders of all the tribes to an assembly near the headwaters of the Onon River in 1206. Here, flying his white banner with its nine horsetails, he was again acclaimed khan, this time the great khan, Jenghiz Khan, emperor of the Mongols and of the steppes. He ruled over about 2,000,000 people of many different tribes, among them some 400,000 Mongols. A coronation ceremony was held, followed by a great feast during which enormous quantities of food were consumed as well as much koumiss, the fermented mare's milk that was the Mongols' chief alcoholic beverage.

One important element in Jenghiz Khan's success was his emphasis on discipline and organization, which far exceeded that imposed by other chiefs. After his accession as great khan, he took further steps to make his army of steppe cavalrymen invincible. Every tribe was organized and counted by tents, and each tribe was allotted its own grazing grounds. Each also knew how many men would be called to fight when a campaign started. The army itself was organized by tens, by hundreds, by thousands and by tens of thousands, with the Mongol aristocracy holding the higher command positions.

Like the Huns, the Mongol warriors and their horses were as one being in action. The soldier in battle wore a leather helmet and strips of leather to protect his body. The chief weapon was the bow and arrow, but the warriors also used hatchets, maces, lances and ropes of horsehair as lassos. The Mongol army in action depended on mobility and surprise, along with individual bravery and complete disregard of death, for its success. Mongol forces made quick dashes around enemy flanks, or charged ferociously, only to withdraw just as suddenly. In such cases, the enemy forces were tricked into pursuing what they thought a beaten foe, only to have the Mongols turn on them and trap them. Finally, Mongol success depended on a highly organized scouting and messenger system that provided speedy communication between large armies that was not matched in Europe until the late nineteenth century.

Although illiterate all his life, Jenghiz Khan recognized that reading and writing were necessary for the efficient organization of government and its administration. Here was another reason for his success in operating a more centralized government than anyone in Mongolia had previously been able to do. After the defeat of the Naimans, an unarmed captive was brought to the khan. He was named Tatatunga, and came from the Uigur, a Turkic-speaking people who ruled an area of western China. He had been serving as an administrator with the Naimans. Jenghiz Khan added Tatatunga to his staff and the latter devised a form of letters to write down the Mongol language. The khan also named a chief judge. He was Shigikutuku, whom Temujin had found as a small boy at the time he defeated the Tatars and whom he had given to his mother to raise. Shigikutuku became the administrator of the Mongol laws and out of his judicial work came a law code, the *yasaq*, which spelled out a strict set of rules for both civilians and the army. Punishments were severe but the enforcement of this code was another reason Jenghiz Khan was able to rule and expand an empire among a crude and nomadic people.

The religion of the Mongols was, much like that of the Huns and other nomads, basically a worship of nature deities. Jenghiz Khan was especially devoted to a divinity that he believed lived on Mount Kentei, near the beginning of the Onon River. When a Mongol worshipped such a god, he removed his cap, threw his belt over his shoulders as a token of submission and bowed nine times. The shamans, who were both priests and healers, were the clergy of the times. The most powerful of them when Temujin became the great khan was Kokchu, son of his stepfather, who was said to be able to ascend to heaven and confer with the spirits. Kokchu tried to secure more power by turning the khan against his brother Qasar, but their mother Hoelun intervened. Kokchu next sought to cause trouble between the khan and another brother. In spite of his fear of the spirits, Jenghiz Khan would not allow a magician to interfere with the rule of his kingdom. He allowed his brother to arrange to have Kokchu's spine broken, thus killing him without shedding blood.

To the Mongols, as to other tribes and empires of the era, conquest was both a means and an end. It was a means of avenging previous attacks by enemies and of securing goods and supplies. It was an end in itself because each group felt a right and a necessity to expand and dominate. No tribe had any moral scruples about starting a war to increase its power at the expense of another. So, with his hold on Mongolia secure, Jenghiz Khan turned his eyes southward toward the northern Chinese empire of the Kin—"the kings of gold"—and the Hsi-Hsia kingdom of the Tangut people, west of the Kin. The Mongols invaded Hsi-Hsia in 1207 and 1209. Both times they devastated the land and Li An-ch'uan, the king, acknowledged himself the khan's vassal. At the time of the second invasion, he also gave the khan one of his daughters. Nevertheless, Jenghiz Khan was not satisfied, for he had been unable to capture the fortified cities of Hsi-Hsia. His daring cavalrymen were of little use against strongly defended walls and suffered heavy casualties the first time they tried to assault a city.

The khan turned his attention to the Chinese Empire in 1211 but progress was slow. The Chinese forces outnumbered the Mongols and the latter also had to break through the defenses of the Great Wall before they could come to grips with the main Chinese armies. The Mongol armies, which are said to have numbered 200,000, ravaged large areas but were unable to capture major cities. After besieging Peking for a time in 1214, Jenghiz Khan was offered a truce by a new Kin emperor and he accepted it. As tribute, the Mongols received large quantities of gold and silk, 3,000 horses and many young men and women, among them a princess for the khan. The truce was broken by the Mongols almost at once, with the excuse that the emperor had moved out of Peking and so had abandoned his throne. The capital was besieged again and this time, in May, 1215, it fell. The Mongols, as was their custom, massacred as many of the inhabitants as possible, seized all the booty they could find and set the city on fire. The carnage went on for a month. After this victory, Jenghiz Khan never returned to China, but one of his generals, Muquli, fought campaigns off and on until 1223.

The Mongols returned from China with more loot than they had ever known, including such hitherto unfamiliar items as silk goods. Every Mongol was rich by comparison with nomads of the past and the khan's nobles could live in luxury. Much as he loved successful looting, the khan himself did not give up his rather simple way of life. He demonstrated in China his mastery as a military commander in the way he handled a large army against a more numerous enemy, and over large areas. Jenghiz Khan also wisely availed himself of the skills of captured generals and specialists who were willing to serve him. In this way the Mongols learned to use siege engines and to capture cities.

Among those who joined the khan was Ye-lu Ch'u-ts'ai, of a people that had once been conquered by the Kin. This man was impressive in appearance, an accomplished scholar of Chinese culture and highly regarded as an astrologer. He became adviser to Jenghiz Khan and a statesman who handled many affairs for the Mongol emperor. Ye-lu Ch'u-ts'ai was largely responsible for changing the Mongol attitude toward cities and urban and agricultural populations. The Mongols took looting and destruction for granted and many of them wanted to kill all farmers and turn farmland into pasturage for flocks and herds. The khan was made to see that he could profit more by taxing farmers and city dwellers and by encouraging them to produce goods to add to the wealth of the Mongol kingdom.

Jenghiz Khan turned his attention westward, beyond the Hsi-Hsia region, to the empire of Kara-Khitai. These people, of Mongol stock but with a Chinese culture, ruled an area in which most of their subjects were ethnically Turkic. Their king was a man the khan hated, a Naiman called Kuchlug, who had seized power by deposing his own father-in-law. Kuchlug became increasingly unpopular because of his harsh treatment of his subject people, many of whom would have preferred Jenghiz Khan. Accordingly, in 1218 the khan dispatched Jebe with 20,000 horsemen and Kuchlug was defeated and killed. The Mongols now held sway over part of Turkestan.

This conquest carried the Mongol borders westward to the edge of the Khwarazm Empire, which included the area east of the Caspian Sea and beyond the city of Samarkand in central Asia, as well as most of Persia, Afghanistan and part of India. Khwarazm won its independence in the late twelfth century from the Seljuk Turks, who had earlier defeated the Arabs and in whose time the people had been converted to Islam. Because of its location, this empire controlled the trade route between China and Europe and Jenghiz Khan had become interested in trade with the west to secure more goods for his people. After negotiations with Shah Muhammad of Khwarazm, in 1218 the Mongols dispatched a caravan of about 100 people for trading purposes. The caravan was stopped near the border and all its members were killed. The khan blamed the shah, although a provincial governor may have ordered the deaths.

The Mongol response was to organize for war and in the fall of 1219 an army of between 150,000 and 200,000 set out, one unit under the command of the khan, the others commanded by his sons. The Mongols were outnumbered but they concentrated their forces at points where the Khwarazm army was weak. A number of cities fell and in February, 1220,

Jenghiz Khan forced the surrender of Bukhara, one of the oldest trade and cultural centers of central Asia. The city was pillaged and the people were mistreated, but only those who resisted were killed. The khan then marched on Samarkand, one of the oldest cities in the world, which Alexander the Great had captured more than 1,500 years earlier. He was joined by two of his sons. Here the Mongols used one of their favorite tactics: large numbers of prisoners of war, taken in the earlier part of the campaign, were forced to advance against the city's defenders ahead of the Mongol troops. Samarkand held out for only five days, despite its strength. To make it easier to collect the spoils, all the inhabitants were forced to leave the city. Thousands of them were killed, but skilled craftsmen were sent back to Mongolia to work as slaves. Samarkand did not revive for nearly two centuries.

Jenghiz Khan spent the summer of 1220 camped near Samarkand where his warriors could practice with the new and unfamiliar siege weapons and also enjoy the fruits of their victories. Wine from the grape became a favorite drink in place of the koumiss the Mongols had long been used to. The khan, on the advice of Ye-lu Ch'u-ts'ai, held court in a manner befitting the ruler of a vast realm, but he still refused to put off his fur cloak and leather cap in favor of the elaborate clothing of the upper-class city dwellers. In the meantime, Mongol forces pursued the defeated shah westward to the edge of his lands. He finally took refuge on an islet in the Caspian Sea and died there in December, 1220.

At this time Jenghiz Khan became, unknowingly, the central figure in an odd rumor that swept Europe and played a part in the Fifth Crusade of Christian Europe against the Moslems of the Holy Land. The crusade began with an invasion of Egypt and the capture of Damietta, a northern Egyptian city, in 1219. The crusaders were defeated in the attempt to capture Cairo and, as events turned out, had to give up Damietta in 1221. They clung to hope of success for a while, however, because of the vague report that a Christian king was on his way from Asia. He was supposedly named

David and was the grandson of Prester John, who, in the latter part of the twelfth century, was rumored to have rule over a vast kingdom in Asia. King David would press the Moslems from the east while the crusaders fought them in the west, and when he recovered Jerusalem he would rebuild the walls with gold and silver. Unfortunately for the embattled crusaders, Jenghiz Khan, not King David, had come out of central Asia and he had no interest in helping the Christians.

The Khwarazm army was not entirely destroyed and fought under the shah's son, Jelal ud-Din. The Mongol offensive of 1221 was aimed at Khorasan, in northern Persia, and at Afghanistan. Balkh, another ancient center of learning, was taken and completely destroyed even though it surrendered. Merv, founded nearly 1,500 years before, suffered a like fate, the men, women and children being divided into groups and distributed among the Mongol regiments for execution by beheading. Other cities suffered similarly but one, before which the khan's favorite grandson was killed fighting, was not looted. Instead, the city and everything in it, the people, even the animals were completely destroyed. Jelal ud-Din, however, was still at large, and in Afghanistan, north of the city of Kabul, he defeated a Mongol force under the command of Shigikutuku. This event brought Jenghiz Khan himself in pursuit and on the banks of the Indus River on November 24, 1221, he defeated Jelal ud-Din. The latter, despite a storm of arrows, swam his horse across the river and reached the other bank in safety. The khan did not pursue his foe further, but by now the urban civilization of northern Persia had been destroyed and the area turned into a wasteland to act as a barrier against attacks on the Mongols.

Jenghiz Khan was in his mid-fifties, still strong but somewhat fat in spite of the rigorous life he had led and the hardships he had endured. He began to think about how long he had to live and what would become of his empire when he was gone. Hoping to find a way of prolonging his life, he sent for a revered Taoist monk of China, Ch'ang Ch'un, who was reputed to be an alchemist with magical powers. Ch'ang

Ch'un was an old man but, with some of his followers and an escort provided by the khan, he started out on a slow, stately journey. It was the spring of 1222 before the two met in Afghanistan. They talked a number of times and Jenghiz Khan showed the greatest respect for the Chinese scholar, but he was disappointed when Ch'ang Ch'un told him flatly that he had no elixir that would prolong life and perhaps make the khan immortal.

In the fall of 1222, Jenghiz Khan began a slow return to Mongolia with his troops and followers, first spending the winter near Samarkand. It was not until the spring of 1225 that he was back in his native land. During the long journey home, the khan had the pleasure of performing a traditional ceremony to mark the first killing of game in a hunt by two grandsons, one of whom became Kublai Khan, ruler of an even greater Mongol empire and founder of China's Yuan dynasty. While the khan's armies under his sons and other generals carried on campaigns in lands as far apart as Russian and China, the khan for the most part was content to rule over his empire, which extended from Peking to the Caspian Sea. He did, however, lead one more campaign personally. It was against the Hsi-Hsia whose king had failed to supply troops as he was pledged to do. In a typical Mongol campaign, cities fell and people were killed so that "the fields were covered with human bones."

While hunting in the winter of 1226, Jenghiz Khan was thrown from his horse when it became frightened and he never fully recovered. At sixty years of age on August 18, 1227, the conqueror died. At the time, the Hsi-Hsia capital, Ningsia, was being besieged and when it fell everyone in it was slain, in accordance with one of the khan's last commands. Amid much mourning, the body of the khan was escorted to the sacred mountain of Kentei where, he believed, Tangri, or Divine Heaven, had once spoken to him. In keeping with custom, a number of beautiful women, as well as many fine horses, were sacrificed to accompany and serve Jenghiz Khan in the next world.

The khan looked upon his empire as the property of his clan, not as a national state. Also in accordance with custom, he had made provision for his sons by giving each of them command over sufficient Mongol tribes to provide the fighting forces they needed, together with enough grazing land to support them, and adequate tax revenue. China, Persia and other conquered foreign lands remained imperial territory. Jenghiz Khan's oldest son, Jochi, had died about eight months before he did, so one of his sons held his inheritance. Jagatai, the second son, held sway over the former Kara-Kitai and Khwarazm empires, while Ogodai, the third son, not only received his share of territory but was also designated successor to the khan. Finally, Tolui, the youngest, in keeping with custom, took over the original land of the clan in Mongolia. He also acted as regent until the spring of 1229 when a convocation of Mongol princes ratified Jenghiz Khan's choice and elected Ogodai his successor. Within a generation, the sons of the great khan and their successors expanded the territory still further, especially in Europe where the Golden Horde of Batu Khan, Jochi's son, conquered most of Russia.

Jenghiz Khan's empire, nevertheless, split into several units and these in turn declined in later generations, except those that lived on in the realms of Kublai Khan and Tamerlane in the thirteenth and fourteenth centuries. The Mongols demonstrated unusual military prowess and a dedication to their goals that not only defeated but also terrified their enemies. Yet any permanent and positive contribution to history was nonexistent, and when the empire disappeared it left behind no worthwhile legacy to future generations. Indirectly, the khan's empire had a tremendous effect on Europe and Asia. The Mongols were foremost among the various peoples of the Asian steppes who erupted into China, India and Europe, especially in the period from 1000 to 1500. The steppe people acted like waves that forced other waves of people outward, to press in turn on those already settled in a newly affected area. Peoples and their cultures were driven, or fled, hundreds or thousands of miles, to mix with other civilizations. Each wave, in turn, passed on some of its culture and absorbed some of the culture of the area into which it intruded. The Mongols, though, were too few in number and their culture was too crude for them to remain dominant for long after they had conquered with the sword.

Jenghiz Khan is one of the most striking figures of history. He was clearly a man of above-average intelligence, extremely strong-willed, a first-rate military leader and an organizer and administrator far superior to any Mongol who preceded him. To achieve this, he was willing to learn from other cultures. His military victories and the extent of his conquests are matched only by a handful of other military leaders. Once the empire was conquered, however, the khan had nothing more to contribute. Every land was the poorer for his coming. The Mongols alone profited, and they not by producing anything but only by stealing their enemies' property. In defense of the Mongols it can be said only that they were no more cruel or ruthless than was expected of armies in those days.

In his personal life and beliefs, Jenghiz Khan was much like the typical Mongol of the period, although able to resist the temptation of growing soft when luxury came to surround him. He liked hunting, drinking and beautiful women. The annual hunt of the Mongols was a month-long event of sport and sociability. As for drinking, he said a man "may get drunk three times a month; more than three times is a transgression." The number of wives and concubines Jenghiz Khan acquired testifies to his interest in women, but such was the common practice of a ruler of his time. His outlook on life is summed up bluntly in his comment: "A man's greatest pleasure is to defeat his enemies, to drive them before him, to take from them that which they possessed, to see those whom they cherished in tears, to ride their horses, to hold their wives and daughters in his arms."

# Tamerlane: Bloodshed for the Sake of Bloodshed

Tamerlane (1336–1405), who, by conquest, created an empire out of pieces of others, was the last of the nomad conquerors to rule over both agricultural and pastoral peoples on a large scale. From a small beginning he rose to command many people over large areas, but his empire fell apart soon after his death. At his direction, some of the most beautiful buildings in the world were erected, but in cities he conquered many buildings were wantonly destroyed. As a Moslem, he spread the Islamic religion and culture, but he killed far more of his fellow religionists than he did Christians.

Tamerlane was born at Kesh, near Samarkand, in central Asia on April 8, 1336. It was told that at his birth his hands were filled with blood, a sign that blood would be shed by those hands. He was probably of both Turkic and Mongol descent, although later it was claimed for Tamerlane that he was a direct descendant of Jenghiz Khan. Apparently he never made that claim himself. His father, Teragai, was the chief of the Barlas tribe, subject to the ruler of Transoxiana. This area, between the Amu-Darya (Oxus) River and the Syr-Darya (Jaxartes) River, had been part of Khwarazm. That empire had been conquered by the Mongols of Jenghiz Khan and ruled by Jagatai, the khan's second son.

Before Tamerlane was born, his father had a dream which was interpreted to him as meaning: "A son will be born to you who, with the might of his sword, will conquer the whole world, converting all men to Islam, and cleansing the earth from the darkness of innovations and errors." When the boy was born, he was named Timur, meaning iron.

No picture of Tamerlane exists, but from descriptions of him he was taller than was usual for the steppe people, being about five feet seven or eight inches. He had an upright bearing and was lean and muscular. He had a reddish complexion and a reddish beard. Even as a boy Timur was a daring and self-appointed leader and became an excellent horseman and archer. He never learned to read or write, but had a quick, alert brain and mastered many subjects by talking with scholars. Restless and ambitious, Tamerlane never stayed long in one place, except for his capital, Samarkand, even after he became an important ruler. He moved from camp to camp or palace to palace and held court in the pavilions of his camp. Where he was, the center of the empire was. Among various sources for the history of his times are two biographies of the conqueror. One is by a Persian, Ali Sharaf ad-Din, and was overseen by a grandson of Tamerlane. Here the subject is called a "liberal, benevolent and illustrious prince." The other biography is by an Arab, Ahmad ibn Arabshah, who saw Tamerlane as "a viper."

When he was about twenty-five, Timur was wounded by arrows in both his right leg and right arm. Most accounts say this occurred while he was fighting for the emir of Sistan, but the biographer who didn't like him says it was while he was stealing sheep. In any event, the leg wounds left him lame for the rest of his life, while his arm and hand were withered and stiff. From this incident came the name Timur Leng (meaning lame), or Tamerlane. Many years later, he met the chief who had injured him and had him shot. When hardly recovered from his wounds, Tamerlane came upon a tiger and told himself that if he were able to kill it he would be successful in everything. His first arrow slew the tiger.

The army and the society of Tamerlane's people were not unlike those of Jenghiz Khan, with some innovations. The main power of the army still lay in the mounted archers, but the army now included Moslem recruits from cities and farms,

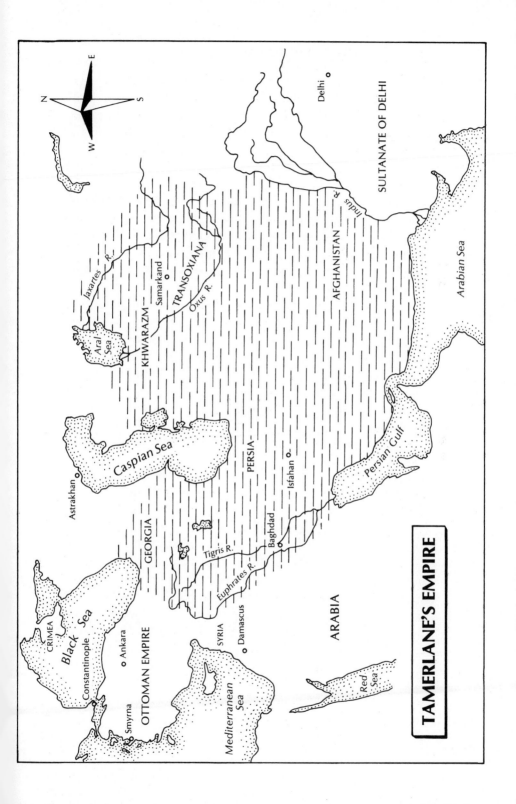

# TAMERLANE'S EMPIRE

Delhi

SULTANATE OF DELHI

Jaxartes R.

Samarkand

TRANSOXIANA

KHWARAZM

Oxus R.

Indus R.

AFGHANISTAN

Aral Sea

Arabian Sea

Caspian Sea

Astrakhan

PERSIA

Persian Gulf

Isfahan

GEORGIA

Tigris R.

Baghdad

Euphrates R.

CRIMEA

Black Sea

Ankara

OTTOMAN EMPIRE

Constantinople

Smyrna

SYRIA

Damascus

Mediterranean Sea

ARABIA

Red Sea

not just steppe nomads. Flame throwers were in use as were stone projectiles, propelled by gunpowder. Until he became old and ill and had to be carried in a wagon or litter, on campaign Tamerlane always rode his horse, just behind the vanguard of the army.

The conqueror was a Moslem as was most of the settled population in the areas he ruled, but the steppe nomads were still largely worshippers of nature deities. As with the earlier Mongols, hunting remained a popular organized sport, even when the kill was not necessary for food. Popular also were banqueting and drinking, both men and women often drinking heavily. A feast might include a whole roast horse. Women were purchased as wives in exchange for animals, household goods or pasturage rights, among other valuable items. A son sometimes married all his deceased father's wives except his own mother. Women drove the carts and put up the tents, while the men made the tents and prepared the koumiss. Tamerlane adopted the legal code that Jenghiz Khan had established and believed that this was a factor in his success, as a civil and military administrator. Punishment for crimes was harsh: a horse thief had to give up nine horses as well as restore the stolen one; if he didn't do this, he must give up his sons or his own life.

Tamerlane began his climb to power by energetically serving Emir Kuzgan of Transoxiana. As a young man, he fought so well for him that the ruler gave Tamerlane his granddaughter, Alshai, as his bride, and Tamerlane became the friend and ally of his wife's brother, Husain. By this time, too, he had succeeded his father and held the fief of Kesh under the emir. When Kuzgan was assassinated in 1357, two chiefs, one of whom was Tamerlane's uncle, Hajii Barlas, tried to take power from the dead ruler's son, but no one was able to win firm control. Tughlugh Timur, the Jagatai khan of the land of Ili to the east, took advantage of the situation to invade Transoxiana and in 1360 he recovered it for the Mongol khanate of which it had originally been a part. Tamerlane submitted to Tughlugh and acknowledged him as overlord, so the khan let him retain his rule of Kesh.

Others, including Tamerlane's uncle, continued to resist and uncle and nephew fought each other in a battle which the latter won. For some unknown reason, though, Tamerlane's troops deserted him afterwards and he was fortunate that his uncle forgave him. He was also fortunate to have Tughlugh Timur return to Transoxiana from his home territory in 1361, which caused Hajii Barlas to flee. Shortly thereafter, the uncle was assassinated and Tamerlane became head of the tribe. Tughlugh Timur made Tamerlane adviser to his son Ilyas-khoja, whom he appointed viceroy. Tamerlane, in spite of his youth and lack of experience, thought he should be the ruling viceroy of Transoxiana, so, with his brother-in-law Husain, he left the court. The two, with their followers, became adventurers, fighting for loot or in the pay of emirs and kings.

Their total force numbered about 60 followers. Each had his wife with him. In a battle in Khwarazm, their company was reduced to seven men and they were forced to flee, finally splitting up. The defenseless Tamerlane and his wife were seized by the troops of Ali-bek, ruler of the area in which they were then wandering. They were held prisoner for two months, a cow barn being their jail. Tamerlane, more and more desperate, one day snatched a sword from a guard and demanded to see Ali-bek. The latter, impressed by Tamerlane's courage, set him and his wife free and Tamerlane began gathering followers once more. Even though he led only a few hundred men, he began plotting to conquer Transoxiana. His intrigues failed, however, and he was forced to flee. Some writers have made the Tamerlane of this period seem a romantic, knightly figure, freeing enslaved people, but in truth he was simply one of a number of adventurers who knew that with luck, daring and a few scruples a man might become overnight the ruler of a whole principality.

Tamerlane did not give up, but gathered another force which grew steadily. Allied again with his brother-in-law Husain, Tamerlane invaded Transoxiana in 1363 and in two narrowly won battles defeated the viceroy, Alyas-khoja. About this time, the latter learned of the death of the khan, his father Tughlugh Timur, and rushed to Ili to claim the throne before others beat him to it. Tamerlane and Husain were left in control of Transoxiana, but they put a Mongol descendant on the throne as a figurehead. Husain was the more powerful of the pair and Tamerlane was forced to acknowledge this by paying tribute. He included in the payment his wife's jewelry and although Husain must have recognized his sister's jewels, he kept them. She died not long after this incident and the last tie between the two men was broken.

Between 1366 and 1370, Tamerlane and Husain intrigued and fought against each other, the former having the worst of it at first and being forced to abandon his own realm around Kesh and Karshi. Tamerlane was prepared to join with the Mongols of Ili to retake Transoxiana. The threat of this alliance caused Husain to offer peace, which Tamerlane accepted but which did not keep him from continuing to plan secretly to destroy his rival. In a surprise attack, he led his men to Husain's capital of Balkh and forced Husain to surrender. Tamerlane pardoned him but some of his followers killed the defeated ruler. Tamerlane claimed that he had nothing to do with this. Two of Husain's sons were burned to death and the city of Balkh was destroyed.

Tamerlane's cold-blooded drive to achieve power regardless of the methods used had succeeded. He was now the unchallenged ruler of Transoxiana and crowned himself on April 10, 1370, with a gold crown. He declared also that he was the heir to Jenghiz Khan and the Jagatai khanate, although he did not give himself any particular title. It was not until 1388 that he adopted the title of sultan. About the time of his coronation, he took another wife in the person of a daughter of the khan. Her name was Saray-Mulk-Khanum and she became Tamerlane's chief wife, although he had eight in the course of his life.

As ruler of Transoxiana Tamerlane had a base from which to attack other lands, which he did nearly every year through the rest of his life. North, south, east and west, he marched his troops and usually won the battles and captured the cities. He hardly ever, however, permanently subdued another state, but had to return, often several times, to put down revolts. Unlike Jenghiz Khan, he had no overall plan and seemed not to think very far ahead. As a result, he never really organized the conquered lands into a settled and properly administered empire to match the geographical expanse of his conquests. He did, though, live like an emperor, adopting the styles and manners of the more urbanized life of western Asia. Banquets and festivities marked every victory, and talented artists and skilled craftsmen labored for him.

Around the lower part of the Aral Sea and the lower part of the Amu-Darya was the land of Khwarazm, which was ruled by a Turkic chief, Husain Sufi. In 1371, Tamerlane took back some Transoxiana territory Husain had captured. Husain Sufi died and was succeeded by his brother, Yusuf Sufi, who made peace. Tamerlane started hostilities once more in 1373 but called them off when Yusuf's daughter was given to Tamerlane's eldest son, Jahangir, as his bride. War broke out again in 1375, but this time Tamerlane had to go back home to put down a revolt. In 1379, he besieged the city of Urgench and challenged Yusuf to hand-to-hand combat. Tamerlane armed himself, rode up to the city walls and called on Yusuf to come out, but the Khwarazm ruler chose not to fight. The city was eventually taken, the people were massacred and Khwarazm was annexed.

Time after time between 1370 and 1390, Tamerlane led or sent expeditions against Qamar ad-Din, who had seized the throne of Mogholistan, an area east of Transoxiana and including Ili, which had been part of the Jagatai khanate. Tamerlane won many battles, although once he was ambushed and barely escaped with his life. Eventually, in 1390, the conqueror drove Qamar ad-Din out of his country for good and concluded a peace settlement with a new ruler in 1397. That same year the successor khan gave his daughter, Khizr-khoja, in marriage to Tamerlane, now in his sixty-first year. Meanwhile, his son Jahangir, who had campaigned with his father, died.

Between 1381 and 1394, Tamerlane also invaded Persia a

number of times. The city of Herat was taken and its people were spared but all its wealth was seized, including even the wrought iron city gates. The following year, however, Herat revolted and this time Tamerlane spared no one. Towers were made of the heads of the victims. At the city of Sebzewar in 1383, he had 2,000 people walled up alive and his reputation for frightfulness and cruelty became overwhelming even for that era. Many other cities in Persia felt his wrath. Tabriz surrendered in 1386 and paid a huge ransom. Isfahan also gave up without a fight, in 1387, but its citizens revolted the night after Tamerlane entered in triumph, and killed about 3,000 of the garrison he had stationed in the city. The conqueror then gave each army unit a quota of the number of heads it must turn in. When the slaughter was over, about 70,000 people were dead and the heads were piled in heaps outside the city walls. Soldiers who had scruples about killing co-religionists bought heads from others who had no scruples. The supply was so great that the original price fell by half.

A rebel prince, Shah Mansur, seized Isfahan and Shiraz and defied Tamerlane so that in April, 1393, the conqueror felt compelled to march on the latter city. A closely fought battle took place outside the walls and Tamerlane came so near defeat that Mansur broke through his guards and was able to strike him twice on the helmet with his sword, but the strong helmet kept Tamerlane from injury. Mansur was killed later in the battle and his head cut off by Shah Rukh, another son of the conqueror. Shiraz was not destroyed but had to hand over all its treasures while Tamerlane celebrated and "the good red Shiraz wine was presented in golden cups by the prettiest girls of the city." During an earlier excursion against Shiraz, Tamerlane met and talked with Hafiz (d. 1389?), the famous Persian lyric poet, who refused to be awed by the conqueror. Tamerlane was so taken by the poet that he gave him valuable gifts, but Hafiz continued to write poetry in praise of Tamerlane's enemy, Shah Mansur.

To the north of Tamerlane's domain lay two Mongol khanates. That of the Golden Horde, which had been the khanate of Jochi, Jenghiz Khan's eldest son, was in southern

Russia. It was also known as the Kipchak Khanate. To the east
was the land of the White Horde, which had once been part of
Jochi's territory. A descendant of the Jochi branch of the
Jenghiz Khan Mongols, Toqtamish, came to Tamerlane in
1376 for support in an effort to overthrow the khan of the
White Horde. The conqueror agreed to help and gave him
some territory as a base, but Toqtamish was defeated three
times by the White Horde before he overthrew the regime in
the winter of 1377–78. Toqtamish felt he should extend his
rule further and set out to conquer the Golden Horde, a goal
he achieved in 1380. After that he sought to increase his
power still more and succeeded in capturing and burning
Moscow in 1382.

In 1386 Tamerlane annexed Azerbaijan, an area in northwestern Persia to which Toqtamish also laid claim. The latter
attacked in 1387 and defeated a small force of Tamerlane's
men, but Prince Miran Shah, the third son of the conqueror,
arrived and compelled Toqtamish to flee. Tamerlane, instead
of massacring prisoners as usual, returned them to Toqtamish,
whom he seemed to regard as a wayward son. Toward the end
of the same year, nevertheless, Toqtamish attacked again
while Tamerlane was in Persia. The emperor returned and
chased his foe north.

In January, 1391, resolved to end Toqtamish's threats once
and for all, Tamerlane headed north from Transoxiana with an
army of about 100,000. They crossed the Khirgiz Steppes, then
turned west around the southern end of the Ural Mountains,
but could not find Toqtamish, who kept retreating. After five
months of hard marching, Tamerlane's army was weary and
short of food. Finally, on June 9, 1391, he brought Toqtamish
to bay near present-day Kuybyshev on the Volga. After a nip-
and-tuck battle, the ruler of the Golden Horde fled. His men
were trapped between Tamerlane's army and the river and
slaughtered or captured. So much booty and so many beautiful
women were seized that the victors celebrated for twenty-six
days. When the victors started home they took with them
5,000 boys to be trained for the royal household.

Toqtamish, however, was a hard man to keep down. He

regained his throne in 1393, so Tamerlane went on the offensive once more in 1395. This time the conqueror headed for Toqtamish's cities of Sarai and Astrakhan, destroying both of them and defeating his foe in a pitched battle during which Tamerlane was almost captured. Tamerlane had now ruined the land of the Golden Horde and gained control of the east-west trade routes, but by destroying its cities he paralyzed the commerce between central Asia and Europe. Toqtamish never gave up. As late as 1405 he sent an embassy to Tamerlane, asking to be reinstated, but the conqueror never replied.

Tamerlane's eye fell next on India, an unbelievably rich land. As one pretext for invasion, he said that he wanted to follow in the footsteps of Alexander the Great, who had invaded India from the west; another was that, although the rulers of the Delhi Sultanate were Moslems, he did not think they had done enough to spread the Islamic faith. The sultanate had been at the height of its power as recently as 1335 when it ruled almost all of the sub-continent, but then a rapid decline set in. By 1398, when Tamerlane started his invasion, the sultanate had nearly disintegrated and the ruler, Mahmud II, was nearly powerless.

Tamerlane sent his grandson, Pir Muhammad, ahead with an advance guard in January, 1398. He followed with the main army of 90,000 troops, but on the way made a foolhardy raid into the Hindu Kush. There was little glory or booty to be found in these high and rugged mountains and the army was almost destroyed by the hardships of the march. Hardly any horses survived and Tamerlane himself had to be lowered down precipices and slid down steep slopes on a sort of toboggan constructed on the spot. By the time the army got out of the mountains, only Tamerlane had a mount. Once they were in India, he found many towns and cities to ravage while he headed toward Delhi in north central India. Everything in his path was destroyed or looted and thousands of people were killed or taken as slaves. The number of slaves grew so large—to about 100,000—that they became a burden to the army, whereupon Tamerlane ruthlessly ordered them all killed.

Near Delhi on December 17, 1398, Tamerlane's army routed that of Mahmud, even the Indian war elephants being unable to stop the charge of the conqueror's cavalry, now remounted on stolen horses. Tamerlane ordered that the city be spared but some of his troops began looting. The residents resisted and in short order the soldiers were burning and killing until the city was a desolate ruin. For 200 years the rulers of Delhi had been amassing treasure, most of it loot they had taken from their defeated enemies. Tamerlane gathered this all in and took it with him. He had the Indian war elephants perform for him and then sent them back to the cities of his empire. Tamerlane left for home on January 1, 1399, having effectively destroyed everything he came upon but without having made any provision for a government in place of the Delhi Sultanate.

Tamerlane's attention turned westward in 1400 when he invaded Syria, then part of the realm of the Mameluke rulers of Egypt. At the end of October he defeated a Mameluke army near Aleppo in northwestern Syria. Some of the elephants he brought back from India caused the enemy to panic. The city surrendered and while Tamerlane discussed theology with the resident Islamic scholars, the garrison was massacred and the city sacked over a period of three days. After taking some smaller cities, the conqueror reached Damascus, in southwestern Syria. Here on December 25, 1400, the Mameluke sultan attacked Tamerlane's army but was repulsed. The sultan gave up the contest and started back to Egypt. Damascus capitulated, the delegation that negotiated with Tamerlane including Ibn Khaldun (1332–1406), the distinguished historian. Tamerlane greatly enjoyed a conversation with the scholar, but he also arbitrarily increased the city's ransom to ten times what he had asked during the negotiations. Many people were killed and a fire broke out that burned a large part of the city. Tamerlane left another center of commerce and culture in ruins, taking with him the city's sword makers and armorers, and Ahmad ibn Arabshah, who later wrote the unfavorable biography of the conqueror.

While in the Middle East, Tamerlane twice captured the city of Baghdad in central Iraq. The first time was in 1394 but the ruler, Ahmed Jelair, recovered it with the aid of the Mamelukes after Tamerlane, as usual, withdrew without establishing any alternative government. The conqueror returned in the summer of 1401 when, it was said, it was so hot that "birds fell dead out of the sky." After forty days of siege and while the defenders had left the walls at the hottest time of day, Tamerlane's soldiers braved the blistering heat and took the city on July 10. He ordered a general massacre, which resulted in the deaths of 90,000 people. The biographer who liked Tamerlane later wrote that each soldier had to bring in one head; the other biographer says two. Tamerlane spared a few men of letters but demolished all buildings except the mosques.

By 1400 the only powerful state left on the borders of the empire of Tamerlane was that of the Ottoman Turks who ruled most of Asia Minor and had conquered a good part of the Balkans. They were, in fact, the one Islamic power that was actively engaged in fighting the Christians. Tamerlane made a sortie in 1400 which resulted in the capture of Sivas from the Ottomans. The city was spared, except for the 4,000 Armenian soldiers serving the Turks. These soldiers were buried alive or thrown into wells.

After taking time out to deal with the Mamelukes, Tamerlane again invaded Ottoman territory in 1402. Abandoning his siege of Constantinople, capital of the Byzantine Empire, the Ottoman ruler Bayezit I (1347–1403) marched east to face Tamerlane. The two armies, variously estimated at from 200,000 to 500,000 on each side, met in battle on July 20, 1402, near Ankara in central Asia Minor. The battle went on all day but by nightfall, with only a few hundred men left around him, Bayezit tried to flee. Tamerlane captured Bayezit and treated him well but he died the following year still a captive.

Tamerlane drove on west in Asia Minor, plundering the Ottoman capital of Bursa and reaching Smyrna on the Aegean

Sea. This city was held by the Knights Hospitalers, also known as the Knights of Rhodes. When more of the knights arrived by ship, Tamerlane had the heads of captured Christians launched at them. After a two-week siege the city fell and nearly everyone was murdered. For once Tamerlane could claim that he had won a victory for Islam over Christianity. In truth, however, his defeat of the Ottoman Turks set back their power so badly that the net effect was to give the Christian Byzantine Empire fifty more years of life than it would have had otherwise.

Another area that felt the fury of Tamerlane's ambition during his career of conquest was Georgia, a region in southeastern European Russia. In 1399 he devastated eastern Georgia to avenge a defeat the Georgians had inflicted earlier on his son, Miran Shah. He took further revenge the next year when he captured Tiflis, the capital city. The king, Giorgi VI, was forced to flee while Tamerlane, as usual, ravaged the city and the countryside. In 1403 Tamerlane returned, this time destroying 700 towns and villages and killing as many of the inhabitants as possible. The Georgians had also been ravaged by the Mongols in the thirteenth century but Tamerlane's cruelties seemed more deliberate. Since Georgia was a Christian land, he could claim he was acting as he did in order to advance Islam.

Samarkand was not only Tamerlane's capital, it was the one city to which he regularly returned and the only one that he built up and improved instead of destroying. In the one more or less quiet period of his life, from 1396 to 1398, he spent much of his time there. Samarkand was a very ancient city but had not recovered from the damage done it in 1220 by Jenghiz Khan until Tamerlane revived it. In his day, it became a city of 150,000 people and one of the world's most important commercial cities. Tamerlane's disruption of the old trade routes between Europe and Asia caused the main route now to go through Samarkand, which prospered greatly.

In typical Tamerlane manner, he ordered a new, wider street cut through the city from one end to the other. It was done without warning, to the distress of merchants whose shops disappeared overnight. Under the conqueror the city also became noted for its palaces, mosques and gardens. The gardens, which had names such as "Garden of Heart's Delight," were open to the public when Tamerlane was away. Two buildings in particular became world famous. One was a mosque, said to have been erected in memory of his favorite wife, with a turquoise cupola and 480 columns supporting the roof. The other was the mausoleum he ordered constructed as the tomb of his favorite grandson, Muhammad Sultan, and which in the end became Tamerlane's own burial place. (The tomb was opened in 1941 and his skeleton discovered.) There was also the Blue Palace, which was both a treasury and a prison. When the conqueror was in Samarkand, lavish banquets took place and the court lived in luxury and splendor. By 1402, however, when he returned from defeating the Ottoman Turks, Tamerlane was an old and ill man, nearly blind, and his lameness was more noticeable.

In spite of his age and his infirmities, the conqueror began to plan one last adventure, one that would be the most extensive campaign of all. He would lead an army far to the east and conquer China, whose Ming dynasty insisted on treating him as a vassal. He would make all the Chinese convert to Islam. Tamerlane gathered a large army and set out in January, 1405, in spite of very cold, wintry weather. He marched his men north from Samarkand to Otrar on the Syr-Darya where his rapidly diminishing strength made it impossible for him to go further. On his deathbed there he spoke to his grandchildren who were gathered around him, saying:

> Remember what I have told you. Be strong. Be brave. Grasp your swords firmly in your hands, so that, like me, you may long reign over this great empire. If you quarrel among yourselves, your enemies will rise up against you; irreparable harm will come to our country, to our religion . . .

Tamerlane the conqueror died on February 18, 1405, while

a violent storm raged outside. For a year after he died, priests claimed they heard him howl from his tomb. They asked that prisoners be set free, particularly those being held in Samarkand. This was done and Tamerlane's ghost ceased to howl.

Tamerlane chose Pir Muhammad, the eldest son of his deceased eldest son, to succeed him as ruler of the empire and to establish the Timur dynasty. He also gave fiefs to all his surviving sons and grandsons. These men, although closely related, did not abide by Tamerlane's wishes. Before Pir Muhammad could reach Samarkand, another grandson, Khalil, with the support of an army, marched on the capital and on March 18, 1405, took the throne. His army defeated that of Pir Muhammad, who was assassinated within six months by his own chief minister. Khalil's reign was marked by such extravagance and erratic use of power that a number of emirs revolted and deposed him within two years. He was succeeded by Shah Rukh, a son of Tamerlane, during whose long reign from 1407 to 1447 the empire achieved its greatest glory in culture and trade. All this time, though, there was revolt within and attacks from without by Turks and Mongols. As a result, the empire gradually came apart. A century after Tamerlane's death it no longer existed and most of it had fallen again into the hands of the descendants of Jenghiz Khan's Mongols.

From Tamerlane's point of view, his life and career were a great success. He gained the power he sought and since he had no scruples about how this was achieved so long as he rose to the top, his conscience presumably was clear. He claimed to be spreading Islamic religion and culture but, as noted, most of his victims were Moslems. He encouraged art, literature and science, but he destroyed at least as much as he created. Tamerlane had splendid public buildings erected, but this was done largely with slave labor, men torn from their homes in far-away cities.

He was a devout Moslem who sacked almost all the important commercial and cultural centers of the Islamic world. His terroristic methods and the deaths of the thousands upon thousands of defenseless people he ordered slaughtered seem more horrible than similar actions of Attila and Jenghiz Khan. They were expected to be savages and did only what came naturally to them as men of the society from which they sprang, but Tamerlane came out of a more advanced culture. As the historian William H. McNeill wrote, he "imitated Mongol ruthlessness as a matter of deliberate policy." "His performance," wrote another historian, Arnold Toynbee, "was destructive and negative," while the best a third historian, Henri Pirenne, can say of him is that he was "a barbarian of genius." One of his contemporary biographers summed up Tamerlane:

> He did not love jest and falsehood; wit and sport pleased
> him not. . . . He loved bold and brave soldiers, by whose
> aid he opened the locks of terror and tore in pieces men
> like lions.

Almost 200 years after Tamerlane's death, Christopher Marlowe, the English playwright, wrote a drama about him, *Tamburlaine the Great*. The first part pictures him as a shepherd and bandit who became a king through his boldness, but the latter part of the play shows how his lust for power and his cruelty undid him. Marlowe has Tamerlane say of himself:

> The Scourge of God and terror of the world,
> I must apply myself to fit those terms,
> In war, in blood, in death, in cruelty,
> And plague such peasants as resist in me
> the power of Heaven's eternal majesty.

# Muhammad II: Conquest for Religion's Sake

Muhammad II (1432–81), also called Muhammad the Conqueror, expanded an empire and dynasty that had been increasing in power and extent for about 150 years before he became its ruler. The empire was that of the Ottoman Turks, to whom the spread of the Islamic religion was as important as territorial conquests. Muhammad was an able sultan, a successful military commander and a man of culture who encouraged learning and the arts. He was also the man who killed and enslaved thousands of soldiers and civilians and who caused Pope Calixtus II in 1456 to add to the Angelus litany this plea: "From the Turk and the comet, Good Lord, deliver us." (A comet appeared that year and was regarded with awe and fear.)

The future sultan was born March 30, 1432, at Adrianople (Edirne), in Thrace, which had been the Ottoman capital since 1326. His mother, Huma Hatum, had originally been a slave girl whom Muhammad's father, Sultan Murad II (1403–51), had taken as one of his wives. The sultan showed preference for his sons who had been born to him by wives of noble birth, but Muhammad's eldest brother died suddenly and six years later the second was murdered under mysterious circumstances. These two deaths left Muhammad, at the age of eleven, the heir to the throne. When he was eighteen, his father made him marry the daughter of a wealthy Turkoman prince. Her name was Sitt Hatun and Muhammad, who never liked her, left her neglected and childless. When Murad II died in 1451, Muhammad became sultan and one of his first acts was to have his servants smother his younger brother. For over a century, new sultans followed this precendent of putting all their brothers to death as soon as they ascended the throne. This callous act was intended to avoid contests for the throne that might disrupt the empire. Muhammad also sent a Christian wife of his father, Mara, back to her native Serbia to rid himself of her influence and that of her advisers.

The story of the empire Muhammad inherited begins in Outer Mongolia (the area that is now the Mongolian People's Republic) in the steppe lands of eastern Asia. Like the Huns and the Mongols, nomadic Turkish tribes moved west toward the Middle East and Europe. The Turks came in contact with the Islamic world early in their westward move and accepted that religion. The Seljuk Turks were the first to establish a dominion when they captured Bagdad on the Tigris River in 1055 under the leadership of Togrul Bey, founder of the dynasty. He forced the caliph, the spiritual head of Islam, to recognize him as the sultan, or temporal ruler and protector of Islam. Turkish rule was centered in Asia Minor, or Anatolia, the large peninsula that forms the western part of Asia and which is roughly the same territory as present-day Turkey in Asia.

The Ottoman (or Osmanli) Turks were the last of the Turkish people to invade Asia Minor and the start of the dynasty is usually calculated from the time of Ertugrul, who died about 1280. With the Seljuks as overlords, he and his people were given land in western Anatolia, bordering on the declining Byzantine Empire. Osman I (1259–1326) laid the foundations for the future greatness of the empire, proclaimed Ottoman independence from the Seljuks in 1290 and expanded his territory, mostly at the expense of some Christian rulers of small territories. Osman captured the most important city of northwest Anatolia, Bursa, in 1326 and made it his capital.

The Ottomans continued to expand their territory and power all through the fourteenth century, including the conquest of part of Thrace, which gave them their first

foothold in Europe. The empire suffered a crushing setback, however, in 1402 when the army of Tamerlane defeated the Ottomans in a battle near Ankara in central Anatolia. The Ottoman sultan was captured and a period of strife over the succession to the throne further weakened the empire. This interlude ended in 1413 and the Ottomans resumed their conquering ways. In 1421, Muhammad's father, Murad II, became sultan but had to spend part of his time during the first three years of his reign fighting other members of the family who disputed his succession. He launched the sixth Ottoman siege of Constantinople (Istanbul), the capital and key city of the Byzantine Empire, in 1422 but was forced to abandon it when other enemies besieged Bursa.

Murad's most crucial conflict was with an army of Christian crusaders, commanded by John Hunyadi (c. 1385–1456), a Hungarian leader and national hero. The two armies met in battle on November 10, 1444, near Varna on the west coast of the Black Sea. The crusader army was routed and Ladislaus III, king of Poland and Hungary, was captured and beheaded on the spot. Two years later the Turks invaded Greece, captured Corinth and established their power over other parts of the land. Thus when Muhammad II became Sultan in 1451, his domain included most of Anatolia and a good part of southeastern Europe.

There are many sources for the history of the Ottomans, the Turkish ones naturally being favorable while the Christian ones, of course, are unfriendly. Muhammad and his father sponsored the writing of histories of their people and empire so Ottoman historiography began in a substantial way at this time. The most interesting historian of the life and times of Muhammad was Kritovoulos, a Greek and probably a native of the island of Imbros in the Aegean Sea. He went into the service of the sultan within a few years of Muhammad's succession and apparently became personally acquainted with him. Kritovoulos later was appointed governor of Imbros by the sultan and despite his admiration of Muhammad, his history ranks well as to accuracy.

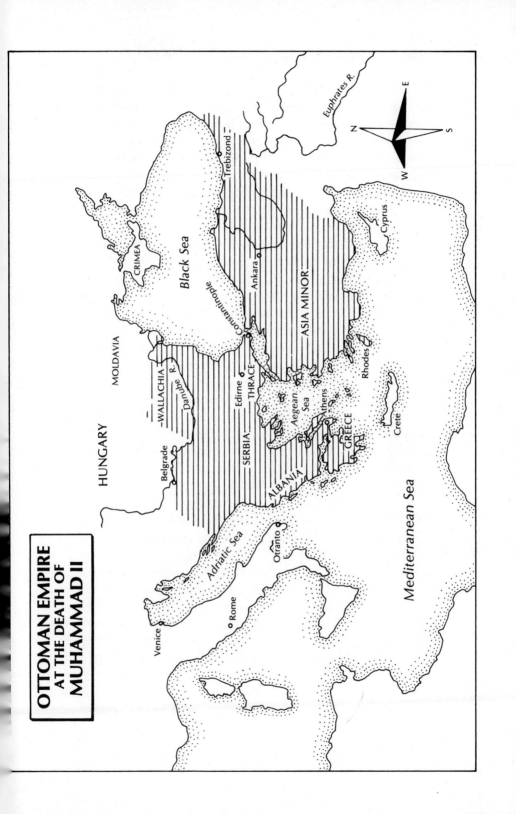

OTTOMAN EMPIRE
AT THE DEATH OF
MUHAMMAD II

HUNGARY

MOLDAVIA

CRIMEA

Black Sea

Belgrade

WALLACHIA

Danube R.

SERBIA

Edirne

THRACE

Constantinople

Trebizond

Ankara

ASIA MINOR

Euphrates R.

Cyprus

ALBANIA

Aegean
Sea

Athens

GREECE

Rhodes

Crete

Adriatic Sea

Otranto

Rome

Venice

Mediterranean Sea

N
E
S
W

Although the Ottomans had failed to capture Constantinople six times, Muhammad was determined to carry on the effort to a successful conclusion. It was, in effect, his first order of business for two reasons: the Turks thought that as long as the Byzantine Empire held the city there might be new Christian crusades sent to help it repel attacks and the city was the symbol of what could become the capital of a European-Asian empire ruled by the Ottomans for the greater glory of them and of Islam.

By the mid-fifteenth century the Byzantine Empire was a decadent shell of its former grandeur, consisting only of the city and its immediate neighborhood. Beginning in A.D. 395 when the Roman Empire split in two and Constantinople became the capital of the eastern empire, it had ruled most of the Balkans in southeastern Europe and most of Asia Minor. The Byzantines had preserved Greek culture and the Roman political tradition while western Europe declined. Moreover, for about 1,000 years it was the bulwark that protected Europe from the waves of barbarians storming against it. And when Christendom split in two, the final break coming in 1054, Constantinople became the heart of Orthodox Christianity. Since 1261 Byzantine had been ruled by the Palaeologus family, a Greek dynasty known for its erudition and its protection of culture. In 1451 the ruler was Constantine XI, who had ascended the throne two years earlier. A competent military leader, a good administrator and a man of integrity, Constantine faced an almost hopeless situation in defending Constantinople.

The city lies on a tip of land in Europe, separated from Asia by the 20-mile-wide Bosporus, the strait that connects the Black Sea to the north and east with the smaller Sea of Marmara. This latter body of water is joined to another strait, the Dardanelles, which on the west connects with the Aegean Sea, and also separates Asia and Europe. In the fifteenth century, Constantinople was a triangular-shaped city, surrounded on two sides by water, the Sea of Marmara, the Bosporus and the Golden Horn, an inlet of the Bosporus.

Founded in A.D. 330, Constantinople became one of the great cities of the world, filled with masterpieces of art and architecture. However, with barbarian attacks on it over the centuries, culminating in the threat from the Turks, it declined in every respect. Including its suburbs, Constantinople had a population of 1,000,000 in the twelfth century but 300 years later this had shrunk to no more than 100,000 and the city had a desolate and poverty-stricken air about it.

Still, the once noble city's defenses were formidable and Muhammad planned long and carefully for what he was determined would be the most important triumph of Islam over this foremost symbol of Christianity. During the winter of 1451, Muhammad gathered as many masons as he could find and in the spring of 1452 they began building a formidable castle, Rumeli Hisar, on the European shore of the Bosporus at its narrowest point. Opposite it in Asia already stood a Turkish fort. The Emperor Constantine protested what obviously were preparations for war, intended to gain control of access to the Black Sea and the crossing from one continent to the other. When he sent ambassadors to protest, however, the Sultan had them decapitated, and when a Venetian ship tried to pass the castles without stopping, it was sunk by cannon fire and its captain killed by being impaled on a stake.

Interested in technological improvements in armaments, Muhammad determined to produce larger and more efficient cannons than Christian Europe had so far been able to devise. He hired a Hungarian named Urban, who turned out just what the sultan wanted, including one monstrous gun 26 feet, 8 inches long which fired a cannon ball weighing 1,200 pounds. After a large body of men was sent ahead to level the road from Adrianople to Constantinople and to strengthen bridges, 60 oxen spent two months hauling the gun to the city.

The Turks were also assembling a fleet, consisting of more than 125 warships and transports, in the Dardanelles off Gallipoli. The defenders of Constantinople were both surprised and terrified when this armada sailed into the Sea of Marmara in March, 1453. Meanwhile, in Thrace the sultan was assembling the largest army he could muster. Wildly exaggerated accounts of its size further frightened Constantinople's population, figures as high as 300,000 or 400,000 being cited, but probably the Ottoman army numbered about 100,000. The sultan and the last detachment of the army arrived in front of the walls of the city on April 5.

Well aware of the ordeal ahead, the Emperor Constantine had attempted to secure help from the west. He appealed especially to the powerful city-states of Venice and Genoa and to the pope in Rome. Neither Venice nor Genoa sent any additional soldiers, but the pope bought three shiploads of food and arms and sent them to Constantinople. The forces in Constantinople set about strengthening their defenses as best they could. The city was surrounded by 14 miles of walls, especially important for the protection of the city on the one landward side. These walls, both inner and outer, which contained 112 large square towers, dated from the fifth century, but had been damaged and repaired over the centuries. Now they were hastily repaired again and the moats and ditches cleaned out. Even if the walls were strong, there were far too few soldiers to man them. A census showed slightly fewer than 5,000 arms-bearing citizens. With the addition of some 2,000 foreigners, there were about 7,000 men to be spread over the miles of walls to face nearly 15 times as many attackers.

Among the foreigners was Giovanni Giustiniani, a Genoese who had already made a formidable reputation as a commander against the Turks. He had with him 700 Genoese soldiers and sailors who fought bravely in the days ahead. The emperor put the bold and gallant Giustiniani in command of the land walls.

Turkish cannon first fired on the city's walls on April 6, but it was not until the 11th that a steady bombardment began that was to last for six weeks. The guns, however, were so unwieldy and difficult to operate that the mammoth one built by Urban could be fired only seven times a day. At sea, on April 12, the Turkish ships tried to break through the boom

Constantine had erected across the Golden Horn, so as to get at the Byzantine ships there, but they were unsuccessful. The Turks also suffered a defeat six days later when their troops assaulted one of the main gates of the city, only to be beaten back leaving 200 dead. A third setback occurred when the three ships the pope sent got through to the city in spite of the Turkish navy. This so enraged Muhammad that he ordered his admiral beheaded, but changed his mind and merely ordered him banished forever and all his property forfeited.

The determined sultan worked out an ingenious plan to move his fleet overland from the Bosporus to the Golden Horn and thus come upon the Christian fleet defending one of the approaches to the city. With the labor of thousands of men, a road that ran as much as 200 feet above sea level was constructed and over it oxen hauled wheeled platforms on which sat the ships. The Byzantine navy attacked the Turkish ships as they were put into the water and attempted to set them on fire but without much success. Forty Christian sailors who were captured were executed in sight of the city. In retaliation, the defenders brought 260 Turkish prisoners to the top of the walls and beheaded them where the Turks could watch their fate.

By early May, a month after the siege began, food was in short supply in the city and the defenders were noticeably discouraged. The sultan ordered two more night assaults, on May 6 and 13, but both were beaten back in the dark. During the course of the month, the Turks made several attempts to tunnel under the walls but all their mines were detected and destroyed. The Turks also assembled a wooden tower on wheels that they proposed to move up to one of the wall's towers to protect workmen filling in the ditch in front of the wall, but the defenders sneaked out at night and set the tower on fire. These events restored some confidence to the defenders, and in turn the Turks were understandably discouraged.

Gradually, however, the walls were being weakened under the steady bombardment and the ditches were being filled in, while the soldiers on the walls were weary and jittery. Following a rousing speech to his troops, Muhammad ordered an assault all along the landward wall, which began at 1:30 on the morning of May 29. At first the assault was turned back in several places, but gradually the Turks got onto the walls and into hand-to-hand combat with the Byzantines. When Giustiniani was badly wounded and withdrew, morale dropped and many who saw the event gave up hope. By dawn victory for the Turks was certain and in the afternoon Muhammad made a triumphant entry into the city. The Emperor Constantine disappeared in the last of the fighting and was killed, although no body was ever identified with certainty as his. The city was looted and the many richly furnished churches were plundered by the Turkish soldiers who slew men, women and children if they interfered. About 4,000 soldiers and civilians died in the siege and looting and another 50,000 were taken prisoner.

Even Muhammad was appalled by the desolation of the imperial city, but he was proud to be the ruler of the capital of what had once been a great empire. He decided to move his capital there from Adrianople and to rebuild Constantinople in a style worthy of the Ottoman Empire. So many people had been killed or had fled that the population now numbered about 10,000. The sultan imported people from all around his lands and by the end of his reign the population had grown to about 100,000, of whom half were Moslems. He rebuilt streets, markets, houses and factories. He also ordered construction of his new palace on the highest point of the city, the structure that became the renowned Topkapi Palace, the center of the sultanate for over 400 years.

In accordance with their usual policy, the Islamic victors did not try to erase the religion of their conquered enemies. They practiced tolerance but this did not mean equality. The sultan kept control of his Greek subjects by making them a self-governing unity within his empire under the rule of their religious chief, the patriarch of the Eastern Orthodox Church. Most of the churches were turned into mosques, including the masterpiece of Byzantine architecture, the church of Santa Sophia. Its icons were removed and its splendid mosaics painted over. Tradition says that at the last Christian service there, just as the invaders broke in, the priest who was officiating walked into the wall behind him, which opened to receive him and the chalice he bore. The wall closéd again and will not reopen until a ruler of the Orthodox Chruch returns.

The fall of Constantinople sent emotional shock waves through Christian Europe. One of the two great cities that marked the rise of western civilization, the other being Rome, was in the hands of the infidels. Later generations, in fact, took this event and the year 1453 as marking the end of the Middle Ages and the beginning of the Renaissance, as though there could be such a sharp line between historical eras. That this idea was accepted for so long indicates how stunning a blow the fall of the city was. Muhammad was called the "precursor of Anti-Christ and second Sennacherib," the latter being an Assyrian king of the seventh century B.C. who destroyed many Judaean cities and besieged Jerusalem.

The triumph of the Ottomans made them the prime power in the world of Islam. It gave them a fine naval and commercial harbor, and control of the passage to the Black Sea and beyond, which was a blow to the merchants of Europe. As an indirect result of the fall of the Byzantine Empire, Russia laid claim as heir to the Byzantine cultural heritage and became the chief supporter and defender of the Orthodox Christian faith.

Later generations of the western world remember Muhammad almost entirely as the conqueror of the Byzantine Empire, but in his own eyes and those of the Islamic world the fall of Constantinople was but one of many events that made the sultan of the Ottoman Turks the acknowledged military and civil leader of Islam. Furthermore, in his dual role as caliph, first in practice and later in title, as well as sultan, he was also the religious head of Islam. The rule of the empire was based on the sacred law of the Moslems. One of

Muhammad's first steps was to reorganize governmental administration so that all power was firmly in his own hands. Only two days after the capture of Constantinople, Muhammad dismissed Halil, the grand vezir and therefore the most powerful man in the government after the sultan. Halil, who had served under Muhammad's father, was accused of taking bribes from the Byzantines to argue against the attack on Constantinople. The bribe charge was probably false but he had opposed the siege.

In his place, the sultan appointed Zaganos Pasa, who did not come from the privileged classes. He also reduced the power of noble Turkish families by confiscating their property. The sultan expanded his own household and most government officials thereafter came from among Muhammad's slaves. Muhammad systematized the various legal codes he found in his territories and issued new sets of laws at three different times during his reign. The outside world saw the Ottoman Empire mostly as a threatening military colossus, but under Muhammad and several other able rulers it also became a well-organized and efficiently administered civil state which was to play a leading role in world affairs for many years.

The firm base on which the administration of the Ottoman sultanate was built consisted of young men trained in the Janissary Corps system and in the palace school established by Muhammad. The Janissaries were the heart of the army and the bodyguard of the sultan, much like the Praetorian Guard of the Roman Empire. The corps was established by Sultan Murad I in the latter part of the fourteenth century and by Muhammad's time numbered about 12,000. It was organized in battalions, each headed by a *corbacis* (meaning literally, "soup ladler"). The most important aspect of the Janissary system, though, was the way the men were recruited and trained. Young captives of war and Christian youths, who were selected each year and taken from families in subject provinces, were converted to Islam and trained as soldiers in complete obedience and allegiance only to the sultan.

Other youths were trained for as much as fourteen years in the sultan's palace school, which began in the new capital. The curriculum gave the young men a broad education for the times, covering Turkish, Arabic and Persian; the Koran; history, mathematics and music; and physical and military training. The graduates, devoted to the sultan, became officials in the palace or administrators in some part of the empire. Conventional education was under the control of the *ulema,* the men of learning. They furnished the teachers for the elementary and secondary schools and most of the faculty for the palace school.

The sultan encouraged the development of manufacturing and trade, especially the textile industry, among his Greek and Armenian subjects as well as among his own people. He realized that by doing this he would have a solid base for collecting more taxes, which were badly needed to support the large military establishment and its constant campaigns. As such expenses increased, the sultan confiscated more property and several times debased the coinage by issuing new coins with less precious metal in them.

Ottoman cultural life was a blend of other civilizations— central Asian, Persian, Greek, Roman and, after the fall of Constantinople, Byzantine. The increased power and stability of the empire in the fifteenth century brought about a more distinctive Ottoman culture which Muhammad II made a definite effort to develop. Poetry was the most favored form of literary expression and the leading poet of the later fifteenth century, Bursah Ahmet Pasa, was one of the sultan's teachers and advisers, although he later fell from favor. Muhammad encouraged scholars, and the science of medicine also developed rapidly. Ottoman conquests, however, blighted the cultural development of other lands, especially in the Balkans.

No matter how much attention Muhammad paid to government administration and the extent to which he encouraged learning, the first business of the Ottoman Turks was warfare, particularly against Christian lands. In 1454 the sultan turned

his attention to Serbia in the western Balkans and campaigns
that year and the next crushed the Serbs, with the Turks
occupying the southern half of the country. Muhammad then
resolved to capture Belgrade, held by the Hungarians, in the
summer of 1456 but a six-week siege was unsuccessful when
the Hungarian hero Hunyadi turned up just in time to force
the sultan to retreat. The last-minute rescue kept the city out
of Ottoman hands for half a century.

Because of internal strife and because the cities of the
Peloponnesus (old name, Morea), the peninsula linked to
central Greece by the Isthmus of Corinth, did not pay tribute
on schedule, the sultan invaded the area in 1458, taking the
city of Corinth after a four-month siege. The next year he
became the ruler of the once great intellectual center of
Athens, which he admired very much, especially the Acro-
polis. A third campaign in 1460 gave him all of the Peloponnesus. When his troops took such fortified cities as Gardikion
and Kastrion, he had all the men killed and enslaved the
women and children. Kritovoulos reports he did this "from his
just anger and wrath," or because the defenders had caused
the deaths of some of his soldiers.

During these years, Muhammad also began his campaigns to
bring Albania, a mountainous country with a coast on the
Adriatic Sea, under control. Albanian forces were led by their
national hero, Scanderberg (c. 1404–1468), who had been
educated as a Moslem at the court of Murad II but who fled to
his native land when it was clear the Turks meant to try to
conquer it. He and the sultan agreed on a truce in 1461, but
the next year Scanderberg, encouraged by Venice, the last
important rival of the Ottomans in the Balkans and the eastern
Mediterranean, attacked Turkish garrisons. Muhammad re-
sponded by invading Albania and forcing the Albanians to sign
a new peace treaty in April, 1463. There was more fighting
after Scanderberg died in 1468 and it was not until the end of
1478 that all of Albania was firmly under Ottoman rule. In one
of the Albanian campaigns, Kritovoulos wrote, 20,000 Alba-

nians were taken prisoner, but some of them "hurled themselves from precipices and crags" rather than surrender.

In 1461 Muhammad found time to take a further step toward the completion of Ottoman control of Anatolia. Part of the southern coast of the Black Sea constituted the empire of Trebizond, which had been founded by the Comnenus family after the army of the Fourth Crusade had sacked Constantinople in 1204, instead of fighting the infidels in the Holy Land. The Comnenus family also furnished several emperors for the Byzantine realm in the eleventh and twelfth centuries. The sultan sent a fleet of about 300 warships and transports to attack the capital city of Trebizond, the size of the fleet attesting to the growing strength of the Ottoman navy. This force besieged the city for nearly a month, at the end of which Muhammad appeared with an army he had brought overland. The city surrendered and the sultan took 1,500 youths captive. He also took prisoner the last emperor, David Comnenus, and gave him and some followers a territory sufficient to provide them with "300,000 pieces of silver" a year. A few years later, however, Muhammad had the former emperor and all but one male member of the Comnenus family put to death.

At Trebizond the sultan found a learned philosopher, George Amiroukis, whom he brought to his court. He also "honored him with frequent audiences and conversations," says Kritovoulos, "for the sultan himself was one of the most acute philosophers." Some years later Muhammad came into possession of the charts of Ptolemy, the second century A.D. astronomer, and had Amiroukis combine them into one unified map of the whole earth.

Before attacking Trebizond, Muhammad had attempted to pacify Wallachia, a region of southern Rumania of which Bucharest is the main city. Wallachia was ruled from 1456 to 1462 by Prince Vlad the Impaler, so called because his favorite method of killing prisoners and others was by impaling them on a stake. He is said to have put 20,000 people to death. In 1460 Vlad agreed with the Sultan to keep his army at home but even as Muhammad finished the conquest of Trebizond, Vlad started a rebellion and led his raiders into northern Bulgaria. The sultan, with his usual efficiency, took an army into Wallachia in mid-1462, defeated Vlad and forced him to abandon his throne and flee for his life.

The more the Ottoman Empire expanded, especially along the eastern coast of the Adriatic Sea and in the Aegean Sea, the more Venice, in northeastern Italy on the Adriatic, strove to contain the Turks. Venice depended on trade, especially to the east, and although the sultan gave Venice and also Genoa special privileges in 1454, both suffered heavy trade losses as the result of the conquest of Constantinople. War between Venice and the Ottomans broke out in 1463 and the former took a number of Aegean islands and some of the Peloponnesus. Venice was encouraged by Pope Pius II (1405–64), who tried, without arousing much enthusiasm, to organize another crusade, but the plans collapsed when the pope died. Muhammad sent an army commanded by his grand vezir to the Peloponnesus in 1464 and retook that region. The war went on for some time: Venice sent a fleet into the eastern Aegean in 1469 and took the islands of Lemnos and Imbros; the next year an Ottoman naval force captured an island that was the chief Venetian naval base in the Aegean. In 1479 the war finally ended with a treaty that was more favorable to the sultan and assured Turkish domination of Albania and most of the Aegean.

Muhammad again turned his attention to Anatolia in 1468 in an attempt to subdue Karamania, a nation occupying the south central part of Asia Minor. It was a Turkish kingdom which had been established about 1250 around the city of Karaman, named for a chief of a Turkic tribe. At one time it had ruled most of Anatolia. The Ottomans conquered part of it in 1468 and the ruler, Pir Ahmet, fled into the Taurus mountains where he organized several tribes and continued to resist Muhammad but was subdued once and for all the following year.

This victory brought the Ottomans into conflict with the White Sheep Turkomans who occupied a territory east of Karamania. Here the ruler, Uzun Hasan (1433–78), some of whose territory included part of present-day Iran, formed an alliance with Venice in 1472. While a White Sheep army moved westward in Anatolia, a fleet of warships from a number of European nations and city-states sailed eastward in the Aegean as though to attack Constantinople. The Venetians also supplied Uzun Hasan with military equipment. Muhammad, decisive as ever, left the capital city in charge of his fourteen-year-old son, Cem Sultan, while he led an army into Anatolia. The sultan defeated Uzun Hassan in August, 1472, and made him agree to a peace treaty that ended resistance to the Ottomans in Asia Minor.

Another part of the Balkans required Muhammad's attention in 1475 and 1476. This area was Moldavia, a region of eastern Rumania north of Wallachia, from which Mongol conquerors had withdrawn about 150 years before. In the sultan's time it was at the peak of its power, ruled by Stephen the Great (1457–1504). He renounced allegiance to the Ottomans and invaded Wallachia in 1471. Not only that, but in early 1475 he had routed an Ottoman army (Muhammad being ill in Constantinople). Exactly a year and a half later to the day, the sultan had his revenge. He defeated Stephen and ravaged Moldavia. Although Stephen escaped and later returned to his throne after the Ottomans went home, he was never again a threat to the Turks.

Muhammad's last conquest in the regions north and east of Constantinople was the Crimea and its tributary area. The Crimea is a peninsula in southern Russia, in the north central Black Sea, connected to the mainland by the Perekop Isthmus. The Mongols of the Golden Horde overran it in 1239 and they in turn were defeated by Tamerlane in the late fourteenth century. The city-state of Genoa established profitable commercial colonies in the Crimea in the thirteenth century and after Tamerlane the Tatars ruled the territory. These Tatars formally accepted the Ottomans as overlords, but Muhammad had to depose their ruler, then three years later, in 1478, restore him before complete cooperation and submission were assured. The Ottoman Turks controlled the Crimea for three centuries thereafter.

What turned out to be Muhammad's last compaigns were aimed westward, against Venice and other city-states, with the intention of occupying Italy and perhaps regions beyond. Fleets and armies, not under the direct command of the sultan, moved out of the Aegean Sea in 1479. In August one force landed at Otranto, a port city in the extreme south of Italy. This immediately caused panic in Rome and the pope and most of the citizens made plans to flee northward, such being the fear that the Turks instilled in Christian Europe. A new crusade was called for and France and Hungary, as well as the Italian city-states, promised to aid in defending the country. Otranto was pillaged in 1480 and never recovered.

In December, 1479, a Turkish fleet laid siege to the island of Rhodes, near the southwest coast of Asia Minor. Rhodes already had a long, 2,500-year history and had been conquered by the Knights Hospitalers between 1308 and 1310. The Knights Hospitalers were members of the military and religious order of the Hospital of St. John of Jerusalem, founded early in the twelfth century as one result of the First Crusade. The grand master of the knights and governor of Rhodes was Pierre d'Aubusson (1423–1503), a future cardinal, who held off the Ottomans for more than a year.

Both the Italian and the Rhodes campaigns were abruptly called off when Muhammad II died suddenly on May 3, 1481, not yet fifty years old. His two sons, Bayezit, the older, and Cem, the younger, both tried to seize the throne. They were about the same distance from the capital as governors of provinces, but the Janissaries favored Bayezit and hindered Cem's attempt to get to Constantinople first. He had enough support, however, to put up a struggle and the issue was not settled until June 20, 1481, when Bayezit, again with the Janissaries' aid, defeated Cem's forces. Cem fled. After another attempt the following year to unseat Bayezit, he found sanctuary with the Knights Hospitalers.

The Ottoman Empire went on expanding for another century. Muhammad had made it a power to be reckoned with in world affairs, but it reached its height of grandeur under Suleiman the Magnificent, who was sultan from 1520 to 1566. The empire later entered into a period of slow decline, with loss of territory and prestige, but the dynasty clung to its throne and its faded splendor until after World War I, when Turkey became a republic in 1923.

Muhammad II, one of a handful of builders of great empires, was as impressive in person as his achievements were in history, judging by contemporary accounts. He was of middle height and strongly built, but with a handsome appearance. Piercing eyes dominated his face, under arching eyebrows. He had a long, thin, hooked nose that curved over his mouth, with full red lips. "In later life," the historian Steven Runciman wrote, "his features reminded men of a parrot about to eat ripe cherries." The Venetian painter Gentile Bellini (1429–1507) traveled to Constantinople in 1479, and the portrait he painted of the sultan confirms this description and also shows a fine black beard. Muhammad carried well the dignified manner of a ruler of men, except that sometimes he drank too much in spite of the Islamic religion's opposition to alcoholic beverages.

Muhammad II was one of the best-educated men of his day, the Islamic world putting a high value on learning. He was trained in science and philosophy and was competent in literature, especially Greek and Islamic, and in languages. Besides Turkish, he could speak fluently Greek, Arabic, Latin, Persian and Hebrew. The sultan gathered learned men at his court and liked to discuss intellectual matters with them. "His energies were keen for everything, and the power of his spirit gave him ability to rule and to be kingly," declared Kritovoulos, who was prejudiced in his favor. He also praised him for the "splendid and costly buildings" he erected.

The achievements of his reign show further that Muhammad II was a determined and able military leader, an efficient organizer and administrator, an outstanding ruler in many ways. But he was also a ruthless, complex man who could be cruel when he thought it necessary and who could wage war with no qualms as to the bloodshed and suffering he caused. Although this was all done to advance the cause of Islam, it seems likely that Muhammad II enjoyed just as much the glory and the power that he acquired through his relentless warfare.

# Ivan the Terrible:

# The Tyrant as Madman

Ivan IV (1530–84), better known as Ivan the Terrible, was the first Russian ruler to claim the title of tsar, implying that his land had become an important national state, not just the Grand Duchy of Moscow (or Muscovy). During his reign from 1533 to his death, Russia extended its rule over land to the south, southeast and east. Ivan, however, deserves little of the credit and today is remembered as a human monster who, among his many bloody crimes, killed defenseless individuals with his own hands, including his son and heir.

Ivan's father was Vasilly III (1479–1533), who became grande duke in 1505. When, after 20 years of marriage, his first wife had not given birth to a son, he forced her to become a nun and married Helena Glinsky of Lithuania. Vasilly applied to the patriarch of Jerusalem for approval of the union because of his divorce and because he was of the Russian Orthodox faith while Helena was a Roman Catholic. The patriarch not only refused to give his blessing but is also said to have prophesied: "Thou shalt have a wicked son. Terror will ravage thy estate; rivers of blood will flow; the heads of the mighty shall be laid low; thy cities will be devoured by fire." Four years after his second marriage, on August 25, 1530 (by the Russian calendar, which was nine days behind the calendar of western Europe), Vasilly became the father of a son, the future Ivan IV.

The land over which Ivan was to rule was a comparative newcomer to power. Most of Russia for a long time had been subject to the empire of the Golden Horde, the kingdom established by Jenghiz Khan and his Mongol successors in the thirteenth century. Dmitri Donskoi (1350–89) ruled Moscow from 1359 to his death and probably was the first to use the title grand duke. He became a national hero by being the first Muscovite ruler to defeat the Tatars (as the people of the Golden Horde were then known) in 1380. A larger Muscovite state was created in the fifteenth century when Ivan's grandfather, Ivan III (1440–1505), achieved ascendancy over other Russian principalities, especially Novgorod, which he conquered in 1478. He also was strong enough in 1480 to free Muscovy once and for all from Tatar domination. Because of Ivan III's marriage to Sophia, niece of Constantine XI, the last Byzantine emperor, and because of the fall of Byzantium in 1453, the Grand Duchy of Moscow began to think of itself as successor to Byzantium, both as a secular power and as protector of the Orthodox Christian church.

Russia in Ivan IV's time had a population of about 8,000,000, which was mostly rural. The farm population included some slaves but consisted largely of serfs, tied to the land and treated like beasts of burden. Almost everyone was illiterate, including the nobility, and such books as existed were chiefly theological texts. The first printing press was set up in Ivan's reign. Whatever friendliness the mass of the Russian people possessed was buried under ignorance, superstition and the brutal life to which they were subjected. If they were obedient citizens, it was from fear. The Orthodox Church frowned on any pleasure as sinful, but there was much drunkenness. In family life the father was as much an autocrat as the tsar was in public life and, in fact, the people were expected to look upon their ruler as a father to be obeyed without question. The position of women is indicated by popular sayings of the time, such as: "In ten women there is but one soul"; "The more you beat your woman the better the soup will taste."

The city of Moscow was a relatively young one, having been founded in the mid-twelfth century, and had a population of

about 200,000. In the heart of Moscow was the Kremlin (from the Tatar *kreml*, meaning rampart). Triangular in shape, it covers about 90 acres and the walls around it were built in the fifteenth century. By the sixteenth century, there were splendid buildings within: three palaces, three cathedrals, several churches, government offices, prisons and other structures. Here Ivan was born and grew up.

The Russian Orthodox church firmly supported tsarist rule and was, in its field, just as autocratic. Its head bore the title of metropolitan, but took the higher rank of patriarch in 1589, five years after Ivan IV died. The Orthodox Church was an unchanging, inflexible force and most of its priests and monks were as ignorant and superstitious as the mass of the people. The church expected the people to fear and obey it but to many of them it also offered comfort and solace with its solemn liturgy in its elaborately furnished, icon-filled churches.

Ivan inherited the position of absolute ruler of this strange, emerging nation when his father died on December 3, 1533. He was three years old at the time. His mother Helena became regent and ruled in his name, showing more ambition and energy than the men of the court had expected. For a while her uncle, Prince Michael Glinsky, exercised considerable power, but, influenced by her lover, Prince Oblensky, Helena had her uncle sent to jail, where he died. She ruthlessly put down all opposition, jailing not only her late husband's brother, Prince Andrew, but also his brother's wife and small son. This capricious regency came to an abrupt end in April, 1538, when Helena died, almost certainly of poison.

The poisoning may have been planned by the boyars, the upper nobility of Russia. Helena had ignored them, although a council of boyars was supposed to help manage the realm. The boyars, of whom there were about 200 important families, first achieved power as military leaders, but by Ivan's time their power derived from their enormous estates. Most of them lived in or near Moscow where they could take part in court life and intrigues. One of their first steps after Helena died was

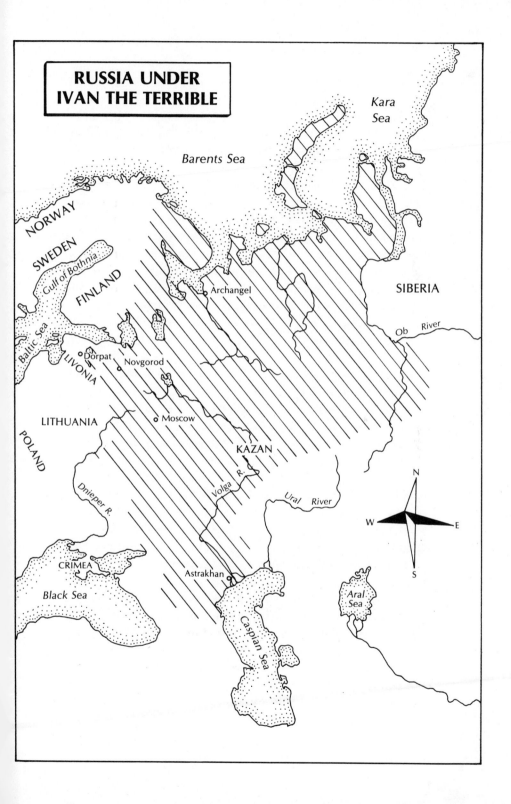

# RUSSIA UNDER
# IVAN THE TERRIBLE

Kara
Sea

Barents Sea

NORWAY

SWEDEN

Gulf of Bothnia

FINLAND

Baltic Sea

Archangel

SIBERIA

Ob    River

Dorpat

Novgorod

LIVONIA

LITHUANIA

Moscow

POLAND

KAZAN

Volga R.

Ural    River

Dnieper R.

N

W        E

S

CRIMEA

Astrakhan

Black Sea

Aral
Sea

Caspian Sea

to put Prince Oblensky in prison. The boyars also fell to fighting among themselves, with the rival noble families of the Shuiskys and the Belskys each heading a faction. For several years each side practiced as much cruelty and treachery as it could muster in order to exercise the power of the Russian state.

On ceremonial occasions, the boyars treated little Ivan as though he were their exalted ruler, but in private they humiliated and insulted him freely and his servants and friends were taken away. The youth also saw around him the daily brutality of the boyars, their fights and murderous assaults on one another within the Kremlin palaces. Brutality toward the masses and the torture of animals were encouraged among the boys of the upper class. Ivan and his friends carried dogs to the top of the highest Kremlin tower in order to drop them off and watch them splatter below.

When very young, Ivan apparently was a sensitive boy, intelligent and, judging by his progress in learning to read, quite precocious. Living as he did, though, this early attraction to intellectual matters was crushed beneath the terror that oppressed life in the Kremlin. The young grand duke learned from the boyars as well as from books. Quite suddenly when he was thirteen, in late December, 1543, Ivan ordered the boyars to assemble before him. He berated them for their misrule and at the end of his speech ordered Andrei Shuisky, then the most powerful of all, arrested. Ivan turned Shuisky over to the boys who took care of his dogs and they promptly killed him. The boyar terror was over, but it was another four years before Ivan's authority was complete and his reign really began.

In December, 1546, Ivan announced to an assemblage of boyars and church dignitaries that he wished to be crowned tsar, not grand duke, at his coronation ceremony and that he planned to marry. The title tsar is a form of the Roman "caesar" and was another way of implying that Russia considered itself the successor to the vanished glories of Rome and Byzantium. Ivan was crowned in January, 1547, in a ceremony marked by much pomp in one of the Kremlin cathedrals.

Ivan decided to marry a daughter of one of the boyar families, which pleased the nobles, and he invited those who had eligible daughters to send them to Moscow. About 500 came (some accounts say many more) and were tested' and examined by court officials, as well as being carefully looked over by the prospective bridegroom. Ivan eventually chose Anastasia Romanov by sitting down beside her one day and presenting her with a handkerchief and a ring. They were married on February 3, 1547, in another Kremlin cathedral. Ivan's choice was a good one, for the couple got along well and clearly were in love. They had six children, but the first male heir to the throne, Dmitri, born in 1552, lived less than a year. Only one of the six survived his father.

As he reached his twenties, Ivan in some respects looked every bit the absolute monarch, but in other ways his appearance and actions were disconcerting. He was six feet tall and well proportioned, but walked with a stoop. His face, with a beaked nose and a high forehead, produced a hawklike effect. He also had a thick beard. His eyes had the greatest effect, being large and seeming always to stare at and pierce those in front of him. It is said that the effects of his childhood hardships could also be noticed: a gloomy, threatening and suspicious expression; never a happy smile or laugh; a tendency to self-pity in spite of his exalted position; and rages so intense that he became hysterical and murderous.

Ivan's pride in his coronation and the happiness his marriage brought him were overshadowed in a few months by a fire that almost completely destroyed Moscow. Beginning on June 21, 1547, the fire raged through Moscow's 40,000 dwellings, most of them wood, and heavily damaged the Kremlin palaces and cathedrals as well. About 1,700 people burned to death, not including children, whom the authorities did not bother to count. After the shock wore off, the people of the city, spurred by wild rumors of how the fire had begun, seized an uncle of the tsar and killed him because they thought the Glinsky family might be responsible for the disaster. Ivan had the mob's leaders seized and executed, but he was so shaken by events, believing the conflagration to be a punishment for his sins, that he publicly confessed and promised the people to rule justly.

From his coronation until 1560, a period of thirteen years, Ivan's rule on the whole was wise and beneficial. With the advice of councillors from the nobility and the church, he instituted a number of reforms. A new legal code was introduced in 1550 and the same year the system of local government was changed in an attempt to give the people some participation and to prevent official wrongdoing. New regulations for military service by the upper classes were put into effect in 1556, while the armed forces were improved with more emphasis on engineering and artillery. The first permanent regiments, armed with muskets, were added to the army. An attempt to regulate the Church's increasing land-holdings was only partially successful. In an effort to improve the arts, science and technology in his backward kingdom, in 1547 Ivan recruited about 120 German doctors, teachers, craftsmen and technicians to come to Russia, but the authorities in Lubeck would not let them complete the trip when they reached that city.

Ivan's two closest advisers during his "good" years were Alexei Adashev and a monk known simply as Sylvester. Sylvester was unknown when he secured an audience with Ivan after the Moscow fire. As though divinely inspired, Sylvester informed the tsar that God was displeased with him and that he must repent. Ivan was susceptible to such fiery preaching and thereafter kept Sylvester close to him as adviser and confessor. Adashev was also an unimportant figure, a minor clerk, when he was elevated to keeper of Ivan's bedchamber in 1543. Within a matter of months of the tsar's coronation, these two men were powerful ministers and the effective administrators of the Russian government.

Like the previous grand dukes, the new tsar was much involved in the business life of the nation. It was, in fact, impossible to separate the ruler's personal wealth and business transactions from the nation's revenues and expenses. The crown had a practical monopoly on wholesale commerce and also on mining and manufacturing. Ivan was probably the largest trader in Europe and he did not hesitate to use his power as an autocrat to purchase goods at low prices. His agents did a large-scale business in furs, hemp, rugs, jewels and other commodities. In addition to these more or less legitimate business operations, Ivan also extorted money from nobles and from cities on various pretexts. When, for example, he failed to kill any game on a particular hunt, he blamed it on the nobles and fined them 30,000 rubles. The nobles paid by fining the peasants the same amount for poaching. When a person was convicted of a felony, Ivan took half his property. The result was that huge rooms underneath the Kremlin were needed to store his treasures.

Ivan welcomed an opportunity that arose in 1553 to make a trade agreement with England. A ship commanded by Richard Chancellor (d. 1556) sailed for "Cathay," the supposedly rich land of the Orient, by going around Scandinavia and reached Russian territory at the mouth of the Dvina River in the far north in late August. It was December before the party reached Moscow and Ivan refused to see them on their arrival. Eventually they were invited to a banquet at which, they noted, all the dishes were of gold, the 140 servants changed their clothes three times in the course of the feast, and the tsar crossed himself each time before he took a mouthful of food and at different times wore three different crowns. Ivan granted the English very favorable terms for carrying on trade between the two countries.

Earlier in 1553, Ivan had fallen ill, suffering from a very high fever, and he as well as those around him thought he was dying. The tsar demanded that the boyars swear allegiance to his infant son, Dmitri, as the next ruler, but most of them were reluctant to do so, partly because they did not want another period in which a small child was tsar. Debate raged while Ivan lay near death, even Sylvester and Adashev siding against him. The boyars favored Ivan's cousin, Prince Vladimir Staritsky, as his successor, but finally most of them took an oath to support Dmitri. The next day Ivan's fever went away and he recovered speedily. To give thanks for what he thought was his miraculous escape from death, he and his family went on a pilgrimage to several monasteries, which made him popular with the people. It was on this pilgrimage, though, that Dmitri died suddenly. The struggle over the succession had thus been unnecessary in two ways, but Ivan never forgave the boyars for opposing his wishes.

As was true of most of Asia and Europe in the sixteenth century, Russia during Ivan's reign was at war more often than at peace. At best there were arguments going on that led to war, or truces declared that did not last long. Between 1549 and Ivan's death, fighting took place at least once with every one of Russia's bordering nations and principalities. The tsar, however, was not a military leader. He took the field with his troops far less often than many other monarchs and when he did he was of little practical help.

An early foe of the tsar was the Kazan Khanate, a Tatar principality that had succeeded to some of the land of the Golden Horde. The khanate, in southern Russia, centered on the city of Kazan on the Volga River. Ivan led an army of 60,000 toward it in late November, 1549. He was besieging it in February, 1550, when the weather turned unusually warm and very heavy rains for eleven days forced the Russians to lift the siege and return to Moscow. Ivan took the field against Kazan again in 1552. After a long siege, during which the tsar often retired to his tent to pray for victory, a furious assault captured the city while Ivan looked on. The commander who led the first detachment to break into the city was Prince Andrei Kurbsky. Ivan ordered a church built on the spot from which he had watched the victorious attack and a cathedral inside Kazan. Even though he played no real part in the war, his return to Moscow was organized as a triumphal procession.

Another Tatar khanate, Astrakhan, was the target of Russian expeditions in 1554 and 1556, neither of them led in

person by Ivan. Astrakhan was a territory around the lower
Volga River with the capital city of Astrakhan at its mouth on
the Caspian Sea. The first time they attacked, the Russians
took the city and installed a khan who promised subservience.
News of the victory reached the tsar a few weeks after the
birth of another son, Ivan, who became the tsarevitch and his
heir. Astrakhan didn't remain subservient, so in 1556 the
Russians took it again and annexed it and the region around it
to the tsar's domain. In thankfulness for his two victories over
the Tatars, Ivan ordered erected in Moscow a many-domed
and many-colored cathedral. He called it the Cathedral of the
Intercession of the Virgin, for he thought the Virgin Mary had
given him victory, but it is better known as the Cathedral of
St. Basil.

Despite some opposition from his advisers, Ivan determined
to move Russia's western boundary to the Baltic Sea in order
to have easier shipping access to the rest of Europe. The
principality standing in his way was Livonia, named for a
Finnic tribe and occupying an area that later became Estonia
and part of Latvia. On the pretext that the city of Dorpat, the
most important in Livonia, had not paid an annual tribute of
ten pounds of honey for some time, a Russian army swept
through the land in 1558. It met little opposition and did a
great deal of damage to cities and to the countryside. Dorpat
surrendered in July and the city and its people were spared. In
1559 the tsar's forces returned to Livonia to create more
havoc.

Livonia was joined by Sweden, Poland and Lithuania in
continuing to oppose Ivan's plan to reach the Baltic. The
leading figure in this opposition was Sigismund II (1520–72),
king of Poland and grand duke of Lithuania, who, in 1561, also
gained control of some of Livonia. (Ivan was incensed by
Sigismund's refusal to call him by the title of tsar.) The
Russian ruler commanded one part of the army in 1577 when
a number of Livonian cities were captured, in one of which
the last 300 defenders blew themselves up rather than
surrender. The next year the tide turned against the tsar. The

worst defeat occurred when a Russian army, while besieging
the city of Venden, was attacked, routed and slaughtered by a
force made up of Germans, Swedes and Lithuanians. More
defeats followed in 1579, while at home Ivan found his
treasury drained by the cost of the Livonian war. He
demanded that the Orthodox Church contribute a large part
of its wealth to the state. When church dignitaries stalled,
Ivan had seven monks thrown into a bear pit where they were
clawed to death. The church decided to give the tsar money
and extensive tracts of land.

During the on-and-off war with Livonia, the tsar also
invaded Lithuania in 1562. At this time, Lithuania was one of
the largest states of Europe occupying land including all of
Belorussia on the east and part of the Ukraine to the south,
which was later absorbed into Poland and Russia. It touched
both the Baltic and Black seas. Ivan was in personal command
of the army that set out from Moscow in November, 1562. In
February, 1563, he captured the city of Polotsk with little
trouble. The Russians seized all the valuables they could find,
including church treasure. Polotsk had a large Jewish population and Ivan ordered all Jews to become Christians or be
drowned in the river. It was on this expedition that Ivan for
the first time killed someone with his own hands. Becoming
angry with Prince Ivan Shakhovskoy, he wounded him fatally
with a mace.

Ivan's wrath next fell on the city of Novgorod—Lord
Novgorod the Great, as its citizens proudly called it—in 1570.
The city, northwest of Moscow and on the Volkhov River, had
been at its most powerful in the fourteenth century when it
was the center of a principality that took in all of northern
Russia to the Ural Mountains on the east. Both culturally and
commercially it had been superior to Moscow, but the latter
in the course of the second half of the fifteenth century forced
Novgorod to accept the status of a vassal. Seeking an excuse to
punish Novgorod for its refusal to admit the superiority of
Moscow, the tsar accused Novgorod of plotting revolution
with Poland. In the spring of 1569, Ivan's first step was to seize

500 Novgorod families and send them to Moscow as hostages.

The tsar's army occupied the city in January, 1570, while Ivan followed with 1,500 companions who killed and looted as they swept through the land. Ivan's son, the tsarevitch, not yet sixteen, was with his father. Although the citizens of Novgorod offered no resistance, Ivan was determined to punish them. From a stand especially erected for the occasion, he and his son watched as 1,000 people were executed each day. Wives were forced to watch while their husbands were quartered; husbands had to witness their wives being roasted to death. To speed up the pace of the killing, Ivan had hundreds drowned in the river. The killing went on until mid-February when the tsar and his army left after looting the city and burning much of it. Estimates of the number killed vary from 15,000 to 60,000. In any event, the city never recovered. Ivan continued west to the city of Pskov, which he intended to treat in the same way, but a holy man there so frightened him with a prediction of misfortune, accompanied by thunder and lightning, that the superstitious tsar spared the city.

The tsar's most dangerous enemy was the Khanate of Crimea, occupying that peninsula in the northern part of the Black Sea and some territory around it. This khanate was a remnant of the Golden Horde and in Ivan's day was a vassal state of the empire of the Ottoman Turks. The khan, with an army reported to be as large as 200,000, moved north toward Moscow in May, 1571. Ivan was with his troops but panicked and fled as the Tatars approached. Stopping only long enough to collect as much of his wealth as he could take with him, he went 350 miles away from Moscow. Meeting little opposition, the Crimean forces easily took Moscow and on May 24, 1571, burned most of it, although the Kremlin survived. About 60,000 people are said to have been killed and the Tatars, waiting only long enough to loot the city, started back home. They took with them 100,000 women they had seized in the course of the campaign, intending to sell them as slaves. As Moscow was being rebuilt, the tsar returned, saying that the disaster was God's punishment for his sins.

In the summer of 1572, the Crimean khan again started north and again Ivan fled. This time he went to Novgorod, sending ahead 180 tons of treasure. He also wrote a will, in which he expressed great self-pity: "I looked for someone to grieve with me, but found no one. I received evil for good, and my love was answered with hatred. For my many sins God's wrath descended upon me . . . and now I roam from place to place as God wills." Ivan was afraid of both the Tatars and God, but he was saved when a Russian army defeated the enemy, killing an estimated 100,000. The commander of the victorious Russians was Prince Michael Vorotinsky. Five years later, accusing the prince of using magic to cast a spell on him, Ivan had Vorotinsky burned to death. As the prince neared death, Ivan raked the coals of the fire with the long iron-pointed staff he always carried.

Stephen Bathory (1533–86), a Hungarian, was elected to the Polish throne in 1575. He was resolved to put down once and for all any Russian attempts to gain territory in Lithuania, Livonia or Poland. He launched an attack against the tsar in 1580, and captured Veliki Luki in September while a frightened Ivan was trying to organize his forces. The next year a worried tsar offered to let the Polish king address him by some other title than tsar and to surrender all of Livonia except for four cities. Meanwhile he assembled a large army to defend Russia against invasion. Stephen Bathory, in September, 1581, chose to besiege Pskov, but a desperately brave defense under the command of Prince Ivan Shuisky held out for three months, finally forcing the Poles to give up.

Poland and Russia began negotiations in late 1581, with a papal emissary as mediator, who pretended to be neutral but in fact favored the Roman Catholic Poles over the Orthodox Russians. When the negotiations ended in January, 1582, Ivan had agreed to give up all claims to Livonia and a ten-year truce was signed. The tsar's attempt to make Russia a power on the Baltic Sea thus ended in failure.

In the long run, the most important conquest during Ivan's reign was the foothold Russia secured in Siberia, that almost limitless expanse of land extending from the Ural Mountains on the west to the Pacific Ocean far to the east. Ivan encouraged the steps that were taken, but gave no practical help. Rather, it was a private family of wealthy merchants and industrialists, the Stroganovs, who sponsored the military expedition that set out in 1581. The commander was Ermak, a Cossack who had with him 840 of his fellows and some other volunteers. They crossed the Urals and invaded the Sibir khanate, defeating it in 1582. Ermak continued his advance, but was killed by the khan's men, probably in 1584. Although this forced a retreat, the Russians retook the territory in 1586 and the advance into Siberia continued.

Besides these numerous military campaigns, Ivan was concerned with his private life and with internal public affairs. Between 1560 and his death, he married six more times, "abdicated" twice, inflicted cruel and unreasonable punishment on many people, and most important of all, created the dreaded institution know as the "Oprichnina," which blighted Russian life for about eight years.

Anastasia died in August, 1560, and Ivan was never the same thereafter. He began to live riotously, his rages and his violence became excessive and he no longer made a pretense of governing justly. Ivan convinced himself that Anastasia had been poisoned and he blamed Sylvester and Adashev. Both were found guilty of casting spells on her and were banished. A year later he married Maria, the daughter of a Circassian prince, and when she died in 1569 he claimed that she, too, had been poisoned. Martha, the daughter of a merchant, whom he married in October, 1571, died two weeks later and once more poison was blamed. Next came Anna Koltovsky, the daughter of a government official. Ivan sent her to a nunnery after three years. The fifth wife died, the sixth was sent to a nunnery and the seventh and last outlived the tsar.

In the first few years after Anastasia's death, Ivan became a wanton killer of faithful followers and innocent people. Adashev's brother, Daniel, was put to death for no stated reason and his twelve-year-old son was killed with him. Maria

Magdalena was a widow who had become an ascetic, spending her life in fasting and prayer. Ivan charged that she had taught Alexei Adashev magic that gave him power over the tsar's mind, so he had her and her five sons murdered. Nikita and Ivan Sheremetev were members of the council of boyars and had honorable military records. Because they opposed the tsar's plan to wage war on Livonia and Lithuania, Ivan was put in jail and tortured and Nikita was strangled. The tsar had Prince Repnin killed during a church service simply because he had refused to wear a mask at a drunken party.

One of Ivan's associates, Prince Andrei Kurbsky, fearing that he might be the next victim to suffer Ivan's wrath, fled from Dorpat to a city under Lithuanian control in April, 1564. Between then and 1579 he wrote Ivan five letters, arguing the ways in which a ruler should behave. The tsar replied twice, showing he had a brilliant mind, despite the purposes to which he put it. Ivan argued that the tsar was appointed by God and responsible only to him. Even if such a ruler was a tyrant, it was the duty of every subject to suffer in silence. A tsar, he said, must be "now most gentle; now fierce."

Late in 1564, after having assembled nobles and churchmen and denounced them for disloyalty and treason, Ivan left Moscow with no announcement of his destination. He took his family, a retinue of courtiers and servants, and a great deal of treasure, including many icons. He went to a hunting lodge about 60 miles from Moscow, leaving both the court and the common people worried and upset at the absence of their ruler. Ivan wrote to the court and the church that since both had failed him he was unable to govern, so he would resign and remain where he was. For all the brutality of his regime, the nobles and ecclesiastics were at sea without the legitimate head of the state and a delegation was sent to beg his return. Ivan—with dull eyes and a haggard face—met the delegation and agreed to return, but only after his demands were met: that he had the right to punish as he saw fit, and that he could create a special institution, a division of the state, that he could manage entirely as he wished.

That institution became the Oprichnina, the word *oprich* meaning apart, or beside. In effect, the Oprichnina was a state within a state. It had its own ruling system, completely subservient to the tsar's will, and in time it came to own and control a third of the Muscovite land. The rest of the country constituted the Zemshchina, the boyars' part, so to speak. The masses of the people at first liked what happened as a result of Ivan's withdrawal and return, for they believed he had got the upper hand of the boyars, most of whom were greedy and oppressed and robbed the people.

To help him rule this realm within a realm, Ivan organized the Oprichniki, a corps of men, many of whom were brutal adventurers. Beginning with about 1,000 members, the Oprichniki grew to 6,000. Each man received some property, even if this meant taking it away from someone else. The Oprichniki were secret police, or vigilantes, allowed by Ivan to kill and ravage as they wished. They wore black uniforms and rode black horses. Fastened to each saddle was a broom, to signify that the Oprichniki would sweep treason from Russia, and a dog's head, to indicate that all enemies would be torn to death. Ivan's fear of assassination and treason was now an obsession and these men without scruples were to be his shield.

What had been a hunting lodge at Alexandrova Sloboda, about 100 miles from Moscow, became the headquarters of the Oprichnina after Ivan enlarged it and turned it into a fortress, with moats and dungeons. Here he not only held court with the Oprichniki but also pretended that the place was a monastery and they were all monks, with him as abbot. Everyone dressed in simple robes and from 4 A.M., when the tsar himself rang the bell calling all to chapel, church services went on at regular intervals until midnight. Between services, however, the "monks" occupied themselves by torturing the many prisoners in the dungeons. Ivan delighted in watching the tortures. Perhaps the worst single crime of Ivan and his Oprichniki involved the Metropolitan Philip, who criticized their dress and manner while attending church services. A group of Oprichniki later invaded the cathedral while Philip was saying mass, seized him and beat him. He was jailed in a monastery and killed by one of Ivan's henchmen when he refused to bless the tsar as he prepared to ravage Novgorod.

The Oprichnina was abolished in 1572, largely as a result of the events surrounding the Crimean Tatar capture of Moscow the year before. The Oprichniki, like Ivan, had fled, both that year and in 1572. When the Tatars were defeated, it was the boyars of the Zemshchina who stood their ground and saved Moscow during the second invasion.

Ivan's senseless killings and tortures went on not only during the Oprichnina period but afterwards. At Alexandrova Sloboda he enjoyed having the blood of tortured victims spurt into his face and sometimes he would do the killing himself. When a group of nobles bravely petitioned him to abolish the Oprichnina, he had them all arrested, killed some and had the tongues of others cut out. Angry with Ivan Cheliadnin, a former governor of Moscow, he called him to the Kremlin and ordered him to put on royal robes and ascend the throne, implying that Cheliadnin wanted to usurp his place. Ivan then stabbed him several times.

In July, 1570, Ivan planned a mass execution in the Kremlin Square (now Red Square). Wanting spectators, he ordered a number of ordinary citizens rounded up by force because the people were so horrified by his excesses that they feared to attend. One victim that day was Prince Ivan Viskovaty, hung by his heels and sliced to death. For no apparent reason, in 1574, Ivan summoned the archbishop of Novgorod, had him sewn up naked in a bearskin and given to the bear-hounds. Once he ordered wild bears let loose in the Moscow market-place among a crowd of people.

Without warning and apparently without any particular reason, Ivan announced in the fall of 1575 that he was stepping down and that a Tatar khan named Sain Bulat, who was christened Simeon when he became a Christian and who was about sixteen years old, would henceforth fulfill the functions of the tsar. Ivan left the Kremlin and went to live in a suburb to the north, calling himself Prince Ivan Moskovsky. The young Tatar performed the official functions of the tsar for about a year before Ivan reclaimed his throne.

Ivan was always favorably inclined to the English from the time of Richard Chancellor's first appearance in Russia. The English, however, were interested only in trade whereas Ivan wanted an alliance and military help against his enemies, especially Livonia. England had no intention of entering into such an arrangement. Ivan even put forward the idea that he should marry Queen Elizabeth and when he got no firm answer he took trading privileges away from the English. He was later mollified and restored the rights. Meantime, he decided that if he could not marry the queen, he would take some noble Englishwoman as his bride and Lady Mary Hastings, a niece of Elizabeth, was suggested. Ivan asked his ambassador to look her over and send a portrait, but Lady Mary showed little enthusiasm. Ivan was thinking of going to England to settle the matter when his death put an end to his English marital adventure.

Among all the bloodshed and disasters of Ivan's life, the worst event took place in November, 1581. He became involved in a noisy dispute with his son, Ivan, the tsarevitch, which probably began when the tsar criticized his son's wife. Working himself into a rage, Ivan struck his son with his iron-pointed staff and five days later the twenty-seven-year-old heir died. After this, Ivan became even more distraught in manner and unkempt in appearance than before.

Although he was only fifty-three in 1583, Ivan looked old and ill and seems to have known he did not have long to live. He ordered drawn up a list of more than 3,000 people for whose deaths he was responsible so that prayers could be said for their souls. He also arranged to have property he had seized from such victims given to monasteries. As he became weaker he had himself carried every day to see his treasures. Early in the day on March 17, 1584, he seemed better, but later died suddenly while playing chess.

Ivan's successor was his son Fedor (1557–98), a gentle and

slow-witted young man who made an incompetent and weak tsar. The ruler in fact in Feodor's time was Boris Godunov (c. 1551–1605), whose sister was married to Feodor and who had been a favorite of Ivan's, helping him in government administration. After Feodor died, the Russian nobility chose Boris to succeed him as tsar.

Ivan's reign cannot be judged on the basis of his personality and actions alone. He was, in fact, much like the Russia of his time—coarse, brutal, lustful. Everyone lived with terror and cruelty and many of the boyars were at least as hard on their serfs as Ivan was on them. Punishment for minor crimes was severe; a person could be put into slavery over a debt. Nor was Russia unique in witnessing such bloodshed. The St. Bartholomew's Day Massacre of the French Huguenots (Protestants) took place in August, 1572. In England, hundreds of persons were burned at the stake for their religious beliefs during the reign (1553–58) of Queen Mary I.

Ivan read a great deal on the subject of theology, composed the music and wrote the words for two hymns and was fascinated by church rituals. No one was more devout in worship than he. He was as obsessive about his fear of God as his fear of traitors. He could not conceal or control his emotions, whether in worship or rage. His violence and cruelty when applied to individuals makes him appear a madman; such methods when applied to the boyars, for example, may have been necessary to maintain control of the government. In Russian he was not called "terrible" so much in the common English-language sense of the word as in the sense of a mighty defender of Russia and her people against outside and inside enemies.

# Adolf Hitler: The Tyrant as Living Evil

Adolf Hitler (1889–1945) rose from obscure origins in Austria to become the unchallenged dictator of Germany, industrially and culturally one of the most advanced countries of the world. He also plunged the world into a devastating war, brought complete catastrophe to Germany, and caused the deaths of more people than any other one man in history.

Hitler was born in Braunau, Austria, on the River Inn, April 20, 1889. His father was an illegitimate child who took his mother's name and was known as Alois Schicklgruber until he was thirty-nine years old when he was legitimized as Alois Hitler. Alois entered the Austrian customs service as a young man and rose to a fairly high position in the prestigious civil service of the Austro-Hungarian Empire.

Adolf adored his mother but did not get along well with his father, who was stern and demanding. He did well in elementary school and led the usual normal life of a small boy. In the fall of 1900 he entered a technical and scientific high school in Linz but did very poorly in his work because he was at odds with his father, who wished him to enter the civil service. Adolf already wanted to be an artist and with that career in mind he went to Vienna in September, 1907, to try to enter the School of Painting of the Academy of Fine Arts. To his embarrassment, he was refused admittance on the grounds that the sample drawings he submitted did not show enough talent. He wrote later that "the Goddess of Suffering took me in her arms," but he had company as only twenty-eight out of one hundred thirteen candidates passed the examination. The following year he was similarly refused admittance to the academy's architectural school because he did not have the necessary academic credits. This was the end of Hitler's formal schooling, but until he became too busy with politics he read widely if not deeply, concentrating on history, politics, literature, architecture, art, technology, music and medicine.

Hitler remained in Vienna until 1913, pretending to be a student or a painter or a writer. By then he wanted most of all to be an architect, but he did nothing to achieve this goal. He painted watercolors and postcards which a friend sold and which brought them a partial living. His favorite subject was monumental buildings; he painted almost nothing with human figures. In later years his enemies said he had been a house painter, but this was not true, although he wrote in the 1920's that he had been a "day laborer" and a "building worker." He lived at this time in a men's hostel and kept mostly to himself, although at times he showed the first signs of a desire to argue politics and history with his fellow roomers.

In May, 1913, Hitler moved to Munich, Germany, a cultural rather than a political center and a city he came to love. Here he continued to paint, both in oils and in watercolors, doing mostly copies of other works. He sold enough so that he could go on studying. Again, he did not mix with others much, but those who came to know him in Munich considered him somewhat of a crank. He could be obstinate and quarrelsome, working himself up emotionally, and also explaining extravagant plans he had for his career. It has been charged that Hitler left Austria to avoid being drafted in the Austro-Hungarian army, but the draft caught up with him in Munich. When he reported for his examination he was rejected as "unable to bear arms" because of his physically run-down condition.

Hitler welcomed the start of World War I in the summer of 1914 by being one of the first to enlist. He was accepted by a Bavarian regiment of the German army. By late October he

was in combat. As he wrote in later years: "Now began the greatest and most unforgettable time of my earthly existence." By December he had earned the Iron Cross, second class, for helping save his regimental commander's life, but in 1916 at the Battle of the Somme he was wounded in the leg. Promoted to corporal in March, 1917, he continued to be in the front lines a good deal of the time until October, 1918, when he was temporarily blinded in a gas attack. Two months before this he had been awarded the Iron Cross, first class.

The defeat of Germany was a terrible shock to Hitler, the front-line fighter. Like other extreme militarists and nationalists, he blamed it on the civilian population and government, although the army generals knew very well that Germany had no choice but to surrender. However, it was the new civilian and democratic government, replacing the autocratic rule of the abdicated Kaiser Wilhelm II, that signed the armistice and the peace treaty. In his overwrought state, Hitler, who was already anti-Semitic, believed the Jews and the Marxists to be the traitors who had betrayed Germany.

The next few years were difficult ones for Germany and its people. The economic hardships and the humility of defeat provided fertile ground for the kind of anti-democratic political activity Hitler became involved in. Enormous inflation in the early 1920's wiped out the savings of most middle-class people. At the same time, under the Treaty of Versailles, Germany's Rhineland region was occupied by Allied troops and the country was required to pay enormous sums, called reparations, to the victorious countries. In addition, in a dispute over the reparations payments, French and Belgian troops occupied the Ruhr, Germany's most important industrial area, from 1923 to 1925. This further embittered the Germans. After 1924, the situation improved. The Dawes Plan reduced the burden of reparations payments that year and the government policy of seeking reconciliation with France led to the admission of the defeated country to the League of Nations and to other pacts intended to preserve peace. Bank

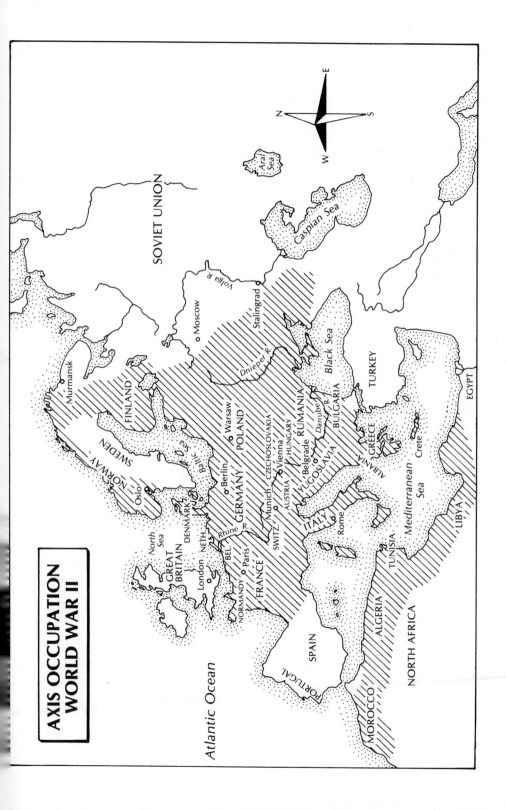

# AXIS OCCUPATION
# WORLD WAR II

Atlantic Ocean

GREAT
BRITAIN

London

North
Sea

DENMARK

NETH.

BEL.

FRANCE

Paris

NORMANDY

Rhine R.

SWITZ.

PORTUGAL

SPAIN

MOROCCO

ALGERIA

TUNISIA

NORTH AFRICA

NORWAY

Oslo

SWEDEN

FINLAND

Murmansk

Baltic Sea

Berlin

GERMANY

Munich

AUSTRIA

Vienna

CZECHOSLOVAKIA

HUNGARY

ITALY

Rome

Mediterranean
Sea

SOVIET UNION

Moscow

Volga R.

Stalingrad

Dnieper R.

POLAND

Warsaw

RUMANIA

Danube R.

YUGOSLAVIA

Belgrade

BULGARIA

ALBANIA

GREECE

Black Sea

TURKEY

Crete

LIBYA

EGYPT

Aral
Sea

Caspian Sea

N  E  S  W

loans to restore and modernize German industry resulted in
better economic conditions.

Back in Munich after the war, Hitler found himself in the
midst of revolution and counterrevolution. The Bavarian
monarchy was overthrown and replaced by a socialist republic
in November, 1917. The following April, a Communist
uprising seized power but was suppressed by the army with
considerable bloodshed. These events further confirmed
Hitler's distrust of Socialism and Communism. This also
resulted in Hitler's first public political activity. His superior
officers ordered him to attend a course on politics for the
armed forces and when he gave an impressive impromptu
speech (against the Jews) he was appointed an "education
officer" of an "enlightenment squad" for returning soldiers
and quickly developed into an effective speaker.

As part of his duties he was ordered to look into the
activities of one of the many small political groups of the time,
the German Workers' Party. Hitler joined the party and
before the end of 1919 he was in charge of its recruitment and
propaganda. The party attempted to combine a platform that
would appeal to the working class with other programs
stressing extreme views on reviving German power and
spreading the spirit of nationalism. The party's name was
changed in 1920 to National Socialist German Workers' Party.
From the German word for National Socialist—*Nationalsozial-
ist*—came the term *Nazi*, which at first was used in a derisive
sense to make fun of this pretentious little group. That same
year the swastika was adopted as the party emblem and
strong-arm squads were formed to keep opponents from
breaking up meetings. Almost every political group had such
squads.

Hitler left the army in April, 1920, to devote himself full
time to his new political career. He worked hard and became
so dominant in the party that by the summer of 1921 he was
able to demand successfully that the party make him its
dictator and not question his plans or policies. As soon as he
secured control, he reorganized the strong-arm squad, later

designated the *Sturmabteilung*—Storm Troops, or SA. Composed mostly of army veterans, the SA at first had as insignia only armbands, but later marched impressively in the brown shirts which they made notorious. Their first victory came in November, 1921, when in a rough and bloody fight they beat up a number of Social Democrats who had come to heckle one of Hitler's speeches in a Munich beer hall.

Under Hitler's energetic leadership and his rabble-rousing speeches, the Nazi party grew rapidly until it was strong enough, he thought, to call for revolt against the government in Berlin. Hitler and his followers were angry because in September, 1923, the government called off a German campaign of passive resistance against the occupation of the Ruhr and a few days later lifted its ban on the delivery of goods to France and Belgium called for by the reparations system. Other groups in other parts of Germany also threatened the government. Hitler believed he could organize a strong enough force to march on Berlin and overthrow the government. He called for such a march on November 9, and so started the Munich Putsch, or the Beer Hall Putsch, so called because the march to the center of Munich began in a beer hall, a common place for public meetings to be held.

Among the leaders, besides Hitler, was General Erich Ludendorff (1865–1937), who had been chief of staff under Field Marshal Hindenburg in World War I. Another was one of Hitler's early followers who later held high office in the Nazi government. He was Herman Goering (1893–1946), who had been an ace in the German air force. The marchers were confronted by a detachment of police, whereupon someone on one side or the other fired a shot and at once many shots were being fired. In the end, sixteen Nazis and three policemen were dead and a number wounded. Hitler was unhurt, having been pulled to the ground by a friend who was fatally shot. Goering was badly wounded but Ludendorff, erect and angry, strode through the police lines untouched. Hitler fled the scene but was arrested two days later. Thus ended the revolution, part tragedy, part farce.

Hitler and some of his followers were brought to trial on February 26, 1924, on a charge of treason. Hitler, who was allowed to turn the trial into a forum for expressing his ideas and his hatred of the government, admitted he had committed the deed in question but denied it was treason. All he was doing, he claimed, was to "undo the betrayal of this country in 1918." He was convicted and given the minimum sentence of five years. Among those convicted with him and who went to the same jail was Rudolf Hess (1894–      ). Hess became a follower of Hitler in 1920 and later was deputy leader of the Nazi government.

Hitler's stay in prison, which lasted only until December 20, 1924, was more like an extended vacation than a jail term. Many of his followers were with him and they were allowed to spend most of their time together, doing as they wished. They dressed as they pleased, rather than in prison garb, and were given special favors in the way of food and visitors. Hitler spent a good deal of his time writing *Mein Kampf*, part autobiography, part a statement of his beliefs and of his plans. The book is badly written and full of preposterous ideas and illogical arguments. Nevertheless, this testament, the first volume of which was published in July, 1925, told the world what he intended to do if he ever got the absolute power he sought. The world, however, didn't want to believe him or to take him seriously.

Hitler's philosophy and plan of action turned on his distorted ideas about race. The Germans, he held, were an "Aryan" race and the Aryans were superior to others, especially to the Jews and the Slavs. To Hitler, a nation of one ethnic group *(volk)* was a tribal community based on blood and soil. The purpose of a state was to preserve and advance "a community of physically and psychically homogeneous creatures." Germans therefore must remain racially pure.

Anti-Semitism was fairly widespread in Austria and Germany, and Hitler had long before expressed such sentiments, but few equalled the violence of hatred. *Mein Kampf* is full of expressions of hate: "Was there any form of filth or profligacy, particularly in cultural life, without at least one Jew involved in it?" Or, "The Jew is led by nothing but the naked egoism of the individual." Hitler accused the Jews of controlling everything he hated: democracy, Bolshevism (Communism), international finance, capitalism, Christianity and modern art.

Quite illogically, he blamed the Jews for what he saw as the evils of both Marxist Communism and international capitalism. His anti-Marxism had two sources. After the Bolsheviks took power in Russia following World War I, Communism seemed likely to spread over all of Europe and, in fact, it became one of the three most important political forces in Germany. Second, he saw Marxism as another plot of the Jews to control the world. He declared war on Communism, calling for 200,000 fighters "for our philosophy of life. . . . We must teach the Marxists that the future master of the streets is National Socialism."

The key word in Hitler's ultimate program was *Lebensraum* or living space. Having proved to his own satisfaction that the Aryan race was superior, he asserted that the Germans were entitled to take whatever land they needed for agriculture and a growing population at the expense of lesser breeds of men. First: "The aim of German foreign policy of today must be the preparation for the reconquest of freedom tomorrow." Lost territory would not come back through the League of Nations "but only by force of arms." Then the aim of foreign policy must be "to secure for the German people the land and soil to which they are entitled on this earth. . . . State boundaries are made by man and changed by man." Germany must therefore look "toward the land in the east." In plain language, it was necessary and proper for the Germans to seize land from the Slavs of Poland and Russia.

When Hitler emerged from jail, he found that the Nazi party, was practically nonexistent and he was banned for a while from speaking in public. Nevertheless, he refounded the party which, by the end of 1925 had only about 27,000 members. A year late, membership had risen to 108,000 and by 1929 to 178,000. In July, 1926, a mass rally was held at

Weimar and here for the first time, so far as is known, Hitler used the outstretched arm as a salute. The following year he staged the first Nazi rally at Nuremberg which became the site of increasingly spectacular mass assemblies each year.

Hitler decided to enter the political fray in earnest by contesting for seats in the Reichstag, the German parliament, and in 1928 the party polled 810,000 votes, securing twelve seats in the legislature. During this period, street brawls increased, the most serious being a battle between the brownshirted SA and the Communists in east Berlin that went on for several days in May, 1929.

The Storm Troops were led by Ernst Roehm (1887–1934), an army officer in World War I, who met Hitler in 1919 and helped him get a start in politics. In his position of leadership, Roehm was somewhat of a threat to Hitler, even though Hitler made the SA swear allegiance to him alone in 1930. Another early Nazi who was becoming one of the party's leaders in the 1920's was short, dark, club-footed Paul Joseph Goebbels (1897–1945), whom Hitler named party leader in Berlin in 1926. When the Nazis came to power, Goebbels became the brilliant and cynical propaganda minister who hated Jews as much as his leader did.

The worldwide Depression that began in 1929 aided Hitler and other extremists because the governing parties, caught between the Socialists and the Communists on the left and the Nazis and other groups on the right, were unable to improve economic conditions. Unemployment rose rapidly and brought more members of the working class to Hitler's banner than he had been able to gather before. The Nazis promised nothing very specific but appealed to the emotions of many Germans who welcomed anything that looked like a way out of postwar and Depression problems. In 1929 the Young Plan, another program concerning the payment of reparations, was announced. While it lessened the burden on Germany, Hitler and other nationalists seized on it to remind Germans that it stigmatized the country with guilt for causing the war. When elections for the Reichstag were held on September 14, 1930, the Nazis increased the number of their seats from twelve to one hundred seven and became the second largest party. The Nazi deputies regularly disrupted the Reichstag proceedings to show their scorn for the democratic parties and the democratic process.

Hitler was committed to winning power by legal means (except for the street brawls of the SA with opposition gangs) and the German leaders, mostly Prussian nobility, realized they could no longer treat him simply as a noisy upstart. At the head of this group was the aged, much-honored Field Marshall Paul von Hindenburg (1847–1934), who had been president of Germany since 1925. In October, 1931, he agreed to meet with Hitler in the hope that Hitler would join the government in a united effort to deal with the country's grave problems. Hitler talked at great length but promised nothing. Instead of cooperating with him, Hitler ran against Hindenburg in the presidential election of March, 1932. He received 30 per cent of the vote, which forced a runoff election the next month. Hitler received 13,400,000 votes against the president's 19,400,000. (Hitler had acquired German citizenship shortly before the election.)

The political crisis worsened in 1932. At the beginning of June, Hindenburg appointed Franz von Papen (1879–1969) chancellor (prime minister) but Papen had little support in the Reichstag and had to govern with the aid of presidential decrees. This unsatisfactory situation led to Reichstag elections on July 31 at which the Nazis got more than 37 per cent of the vote and 230 out of 608 seats in the legislature. Hitler's party was now the strongest. The next month Hitler was offered the vice chancellorship but refused, determined to have all or nothing. In November another election was held and this time the Nazis lost 2,000,000 votes and some seats but still remained the largest party. The election campaign was marked by much violence, mostly perpetrated by the SA. Five hundred clashes in Prussia left nearly a hundred people dead and more than a thousand wounded, while seventeen were killed in Hamburg.

With Papen unable to govern, on December 3 Hindenburg named Kurt von Schleicher (1882–1934) to be chancellor. Schleicher was a leading army general both during and after the world war and he and Papen, especially the latter, had a great deal of influence over the aging Hindenburg, who was becoming senile. Schleicher could not govern either and resigned on January 28. It was clear that Hitler and the Nazis would have to be admitted to power to avoid revolution but Papen and Schleicher, although at odds with one another, thought they could control the actions of the former corporal of low origin. At last, on January 30, 1933, Hitler was named chancellor, with Papen as vice chancellor.

Hitler's assumption of the most important post in the government was received with various emotions in Germany. Liberals were horrified, but many people, regardless of politics, were so disillusioned by the governmental incompetence and political bickering of recent years that they welcomed what they sensed would be a complete change. At least there might be public order and an end to confusion in government. Some observers felt that Germany was returning to its natural condition of government—autocratic, if not dictatorial, rule rather than democracy, which seemed to have failed. The Nazis, of course, were jubilant and the brownshirted Storm Troopers paraded boisterously through the streets.

Hitler had become head of the government without either a revolution or a clear-cut victory in elections. He still was not taken seriously in some circles and many expected him to fail. At the least, they did not think he would be able to impose a dictatorship. Hitler, however, knew exactly what he wanted— absolute power. To secure this he took steps to keep the army, always a major influence in Germany, friendly, and he let it be known that he intended to ignore the restrictions of the Treaty of Versailles and would rearm the nation. He intended to get rid of the treaty in one way or another, to unite Austria with Germany, to incorporate into the Reich the German-populated area of Czechoslovakia and, eventually, to seize land to the east for Germany's growing population.

In less than a month the Nazis demonstrated both their lack of scruples and their cleverness in using events to their advantage. On February 27, 1933, the Reichstag building was set on fire and the police arrested on the spot a Dutch Communist named van der Lubbe. There seemed little doubt that he started the fire, probably on his own, but the Nazis immediately charged that it had been instigated by the Communist party as the signal for a revolutionary uprising. The day after the fire, Hitler prevailed on Hindenburg to sign a decree that suspended all guarantees of personal liberty, such as freedom of the press, and increased the penalties for many crimes. In effect, the Nazis could now do as they wished in the way they treated opponents.

In 1933 Hitler moved rapidly to consolidate further his power. He called an election for March, 1933, in which the Nazis polled 43.9 per cent of the vote, again failing to get a majority in the legislature. However, the Nazis joined with some nationalist groups, and were able to pass an act that gave the government the power to make laws without going through the Reichstag and laws that need not conform to the nation's constitution. This power was to be for a five-year period, and it was all Hitler needed to become a complete dictator. In May all the property of the Social Democratic party was confiscated. Shortly after, all radio broadcasting and newspaper publishing were placed under the control of the government and the Nazi party.

Also in May the world witnessed the Nazis' contempt for learning and their intention to try to destroy any writings with which they disagreed. With students leading a midnight march, a pile of books, estimated at 20,000 volumes, was set on fire in front of the University of Berlin. Works by world-famous authors, German and others, were included. As the books burned, Goebbels declared: "These flames not only illuminate the final end of an old era; they also light up the new."

In foreign policy, Hitler's first move came in October, 1933, when he announced that Germany was withdrawing from the international disarmament conference, the sessions of which were held in Geneva, Switzerland, and from the League of Nations. Calling a plebiscite to endorse this move, Hitler received 95 per cent of the vote.

By the end of their first year in office, the Nazis had abolished the trade unions and merged them into one government-controlled German Labor Front. Finally, all political parties were banned—except the Nazis. The process of taking control was marked by violence. Goering was minister of the interior of Prussia, which gave him police power over about two-thirds of Germany. He turned the SA into auxiliary police and allowed them to beat up anyone they wished. Concentration camps were set up to imprison those persons the Nazis considered enemies, while the civil service was purged of Jews.

Hitler ran into difficulties in his own ranks in 1934. The SA, swollen in numbers, had become less important than before victory was won and was unhappy with its lot. Its head, Ernst Roehm, was pushing for more power. He wanted to incorporate the Storm Troopers into the regular army with himself, presumably, as head. On the other hand, there was considerable criticism of Roehm and other SA leaders for their luxurious life style and their obvious homosexuality. On the grounds that Roehm was plotting to overthrow him, Hitler struck on June 30, 1934, ordering Roehm and others executed out of hand. The dead included Schleicher and Gregor Strasser (1892–1934). Strasser, an early Nazi, represented the radical wing of the party which thought that socialism and nationalism could work together. Hitler, however, never had any real interest in socialism. Defending his actions, which had resulted in about 400 deaths in all, in a speech that lasted seven hours, Hitler declared: "If anyone raises his hand to strike the state, then certain death is his lot."

With the downgrading of the SA, the blackshirted SS (Schutzstaffel) came to the fore. This elite troop had been a small unit acting as Hitler's bodyguard when Heinrich Himmler (1900–45) was made its chief in 1929. Himmler was another early Nazi and rabid racist who took part in the 1923 putsch. Under him, the size and importance of the SS increased. Goering, meanwhile, organized the Gestapo as the Prussian political police. The Gestapo was placed under Himmler as part of the SS in 1936 and these two organizations were responsible for most of the tortures and other atrocities, in and out of concentration camps, in the Nazi era.

The old military hero Hindenburg died on August 2, 1934. Almost at once Hitler proclaimed that the office of president would be merged with that of chancellor and that he was now Head of State and Supreme Commander of the Armed Forces (a ceremonial title that went with the office of president). Hitler was without question *der Führer,* the leader. "Heil, Hitler," shouted with outstretched arm, became a common greeting and salute.

In March, 1935, Hitler announced that military conscription would be reintroduced and that the German army would be built up to thirty-six divisions and 550,000 men. Under the Treaty of Versailles, Germany was supposed to have only 100,000 soldiers. He also began a naval building program and recreated the air force, which was banned entirely under the treaty. A year later, he ordered the army to move into the Rhineland area, which Germany had been forbidden to militarize or fortify under the treaty. Even the German generals expected France and England to react with force, but nothing happened beyond some useless protests. Hitler, whose judgment in those days was surer than that of his generals, estimated the mood of the western democracies correctly. They wanted peace at any price and most people were reluctant to look beyond their immediate material interests. At the beginning of 1938 the Führer took direct control of the armed forces as commander-in-chief, forcing out some generals who were reluctant to subordinate themselves to a man they still looked down on socially.

When civil war broke out in Spain in July, 1936, between the Republican government and the rebel Fascist forces under General Francisco Franco, Hitler offered aid to the rebels. Spain proved a valuable testing ground for the new German air force and for tanks and other military equipment.

In October Hitler signed a treaty of alliance, to form the

Rome-Berlin Axis, with Benito Mussolini (1883–1945), known as Il Duce, who had headed the dictatorial Fascist government of Italy since 1922. A month later came the signing of a treaty with Japan, called the Anti-Comintern Pact because it was supposedly aimed at international Communism. The general alliance with Italy was turned into a military agreement in May, 1939, and the two dictators hailed it as a "Pact of Steel."

Hitler had made no secret of his plan to join Austria with Germany and in early 1938 he took steps to achieve this. In February, he presented Kurt von Schuschnigg (1897–      ), the Austrian chancellor, with demands that he lift the ban on the Austrian Nazi party and that he make Arthur Seyss-Inquart (1892–1946), an Austrian Nazi, minister of the interior, which would give him control of the national police. Schuschnigg had no choice but to agree. On March 12, Hitler ordered German troops into Austria and declared it part of Germany. Hitler followed his troops and was hailed by the Nazis of his native land.

The merger of Austria into the Reich was but the first step in a planned program of German expansion. Hitler next turned his attention to the Sudetenland, a part of Czechoslovakia inhabited by a large number of Germans. The Führer asserted they were being mistreated and demanded better status for them from the Czechs. A Nazi party among the Sudeten Germans helped stir up trouble. By September it was clear that Hitler would invade Czechoslovakia unless his demands were met. Prime Minister Neville Chamberlain (1869–1940) of Great Britain twice flew to Germany to try to work out a compromise but Hitler would not relent. He sensed that Britain and France would not go to war over such an issue. The leaders of Germany, Italy, Great Britain and France met at Munich on September 29 and the democracies gave in. They advised the Czechs to meet Hitler's terms, which were to surrender the Sudetenland, which in turn meant surrendering their strongest defense line. The German army marched in and the Munich Pact became a symbol of the policy of appeasement, of giving in to the demands of dictators.

Inside Germany Hitler was carrying out another part of his program, the one that obsessed him most: the persecution of the Jews. The Nuremberg Laws were enacted in September, 1935, depriving Germans of Jewish blood of their citizenship and forbidding marriage between Germans and Jews and the employment of German servants by Jews. On the night of November 9, 1938, the first full-scale pogrom was unleashed throughout Germany. Homes, shops and synagogues were burned, a number of Jews were killed or injured and 20,000 were seized and sent to concentration camps.

After the Munich Pact, events moved ever faster and always in the direction of war. In March, 1939, in violation of the Munich agreement, Hitler's army invaded and took over the rest of Czechoslovakia. Great Britain and France, finally aroused to the menace of Hitlerism, were rearming and Britain signed a mutual assistance treaty with Poland. Both Germany and the western allies were negotiating with Soviet Russia, the hesitant democracries showing distaste for the process. Hitler, with his usual lack of scruples, in late August, 1939, surprised the world by reaching an agreement with Joseph Stalin, presumably his arch enemy as the ruler of international Communism, against which Hitler had so often raved.

With Russia neutralized and still believing that the western democracies would not fight, Hitler ordered the invasion of Poland on September 1. Within two weeks the German air force and the mechanized ground forces destroyed the old-fashioned Polish army. The world saw its first example of *Blitzkrieg*—"lightning war." Russia moved in to occupy some of eastern Poland while Great Britain and France declared war on Germany but were unable to give the Poles any practical aid.

The German generals were surprised at the ease with which they had defeated Poland, but they were more wary of attacking the British and French in the west, which meant assaulting the seemingly strong fortifications of the French Maginot Line. Hitler, however, ordered that an offensive be planned for November. The generals stalled, the weather turned bad and eventually the attack was called off. There was no more fighting in 1939.

The period of inactivity in western Europe ended abruptly on April 9, 1940, when German troops invaded Denmark and Norway. Denmark was conquered in a matter of hours and Norway within two months, by which time the British troops who had been landed there to drive out the Germans were defeated and evacuated. Hitler thereby not only kept the allies out of Scandinavia but also protected the route over which Swedish iron ore came to Germany.

Even before Norway was fully conquered, Hitler ordered an all-out attack on the French and British lines in France to begin May 10. The advance started with eighty-nine German divisions, backed by dive bombers and at least 1,000 tanks. Parachute and glider troops were used on a large scale for the first time to take strong points behind the front. The German high command had proposed that the main attack be from the north, through the Netherlands and Belgium. Hitler, however, approved a plan his generals considered risky. He would send the main force through the Ardennes region of northeastern France, an area thought impossible for tank maneuvers. Again Hitler proved to be right. The French front was easily broken and the German army swept to the coast and the English Channel in ten days. British forces were surrounded at Dunkirk on the Channel and only an extraordinary effort by the British navy and many amateur sailors rescued 338,000 men and took them to Britain. Luxembourg, the Netherlands and Belgium were occupied and on June 22 France signed an armistice. The western powers were defeated and out of the war, except for Great Britain.

Britain expected an invasion in the near future and Hitler ordered preparations started, although the process was carried out rather half-heartedly. The high command feared the British navy, and Hitler still held hopes of inducing the British to sue for peace. In any event, no invasion ever took place but in August, 1940, the German air force—the *Luftwaffe*—began massive bombing raids on Great Britain.

In the early part of 1941, with plans in the making for the invasion of Russia, Hitler turned his attention to the Balkans. He wanted to secure his southeastern flank and he also had to go to the rescue of his ally Mussolini.

Striving to copy his fellow dictator, Il Duce invaded Greece in October, 1940. Unfortunately for the Italian dictator's prestige, the Greeks defeated the Italians. On February 28, Hitler occupied Hungary, an ally, the German troops moving on into Rumania and Bulgaria. The Yugoslavian government was pressured into signing a treaty with Hitler but a revolt overturned the government and repudiated the pact. Hitler expressed his fury not only by invading the country but also by heavily and unnecessarily bombing Belgrade. Yugoslavia succumbed on April 17 and six days later German troops forced Greece to surrender also. The German tide rolled on as parachute troops drove the British off the island of Crete in the Mediterranean Sea while other units went to North Africa to bolster Mussolini's forces, which had been soundly trounced there also.

Despite his treaty of neutrality with Russia, Hitler had always intended sooner or later to attack the Soviet Union to seize the *Lebensraum* he so often talked about. On June 22, 1941, the most massive attack in military history was launched by the German army along the entire Russian frontier. Caught by surprise, the Russian army reeled backward, giving up enormous amounts of territory and hundreds of thousands of prisoners. In a few weeks the Germans were sure the war was nearly over, but more and more Russian troops appeared to take the places of those killed or captured. Moscow appeared about to fall when the German advance began to slow down. On December 6, with winter setting in and the German army without proper clothing for the season, the Russians, to Hitler's amazement and consternation, launched a counterattack. Despite the pleading of the generals, the Führer refused to allow his troops to withdraw and to consolidate their lines in better defensive position. They stopped the Russians only after being badly battered. Hitler, who had talked of letting the Russians starve to death and of destroying the city of

Leningrad and all its people, was defeated for the first time. This also marked his first serious disagreement with the generals and in December he announced that he was taking over command of the army.

Another significant turning point in the war occurred on December 7, 1941, when the Japanese fleet's warplanes attacked the American naval base at Pearl Harbor, Hawaii, bringing the United States into the war. Hitler, in support of his Japanese allies, declared war on America, apparently believing that in view of the aid the United States was already giving Britain, war was inevitable.

In the summer of 1942, Hitler launched another offensive against Russia, directed mostly toward the southeast, and for a while the German army rolled forward as before. By late summer, the Führer ruled over the greatest extent of territory he was ever to conquer, from the Atlantic Ocean to the Volga River and from Norway to North Africa.

By autumn, however, the tide turned. In October the German North African army was defeated by the British and in early November British and American troops occupied French North Africa. Later that month the Russians launched another counterattack north and south of Stalingrad (now Volgograd) on the Volga, where the German advance had ground to a halt. Hitler lost the initiative and never regained the military momentum his earlier attacks generated. He also began to lose his sense of what would succeed and what wouldn't, becoming simply stubborn and unrealistic as to what could be asked of even the excellent German army. At Stalingrad he refused to let the troops retreat while they could, insisting they fight to the death. As a result, what was left of this army, 90,000 officers and men, including a field marshal, surrendered on January 31, 1943, after a brave and stubborn resistance. The next day, with no concern for the men he had condemned to death, Hitler raved about the ingratitude and disloyalty of the officers at Stalingrad.

Nazi Germany's fortunes declined still further in 1943. The U-boat campaign against vital allied merchant shipping in the

Atlantic, which had nearly brought defeat to Britain earlier, was no longer effective. Hitler was particularly incensed because his submarines could not stop the Allied convoys carrying supplies to Russia by the Arctic route to Murmansk. At the same time, Allied air attacks on German cities and industrial centers increased, the Americans bombing by day while the British continued to bomb by night. Hitler, incidentally, refused to visit his bombed cities, except for infrequent trips to Berlin. Nor could he bear to see wounded soldiers. Mussolini's Fascist dictatorship was overthrown in July and Il Duce arrested. Hitler had him rescued two months later in a daring operation by glider troops, but Mussolini was no longer of any importance in world affairs.

The Allied landing on the beaches of Normandy on June 6, 1944, and the fighting that followed the rest of that year demonstrated both the slow but sure defeat in store for Germany and the increasingly unrealistic view of the situation taken by Hitler. He refused to let the generals meet the Normandy landings as they thought best but dismissed some of them when they could not prevent the invasion from being successful. When the Americans broke through the German lines at the end of July, sound military judgment called for a withdrawal behind the Seine River but the Führer, far away at his headquarters in East Prussia, not only refused but ordered a counterattack. Meanwhile, the Russians in another offensive were advancing into Poland and moving steadily toward Germany. Here, too, Hitler refused to allow any troops anywhere to withdraw an inch.

A number of attempts were made, or planned, on Hitler's life over the years. In several cases he claimed that providence had saved him for his historic destiny. The attempt that came nearest to succeeding took place on July 20, 1944, in his East Prussian headquarters. A German officer, one of the leaders of a plot to rid Germany of Hitler, placed a briefcase with a bomb in it under a conference table. The table had very heavy legs which absorbed most of the blast when the bomb went off. Hitler's clothes were torn and his hair was scorched, one arm made stiff and a leg burned, but he was not seriously hurt. The plotters were rounded up and executed.

The tide continued to go against Germany in the fall of 1944. Russia forced Rumania and Bulgaria out of the war and in October the British freed Athens and the Russians reached Belgrade. Nevertheless, Hitler decided on one more offensive in the west. In great secrecy the Germans massed a strong force that was to attack through the Ardennes, across the Meuse River, and capture Antwerp, Belgium, the Allies' principal supply port. The attack was launched on December 12 and for two weeks the Germans drove the Allies back in the Battle of the Bulge. By the beginning of January, however, Allied superiority in tanks, planes and men asserted itself and the Germans withdrew defeated.

While Hitler was battling his external enemies, he was waging an even more horrible war against those he hated the most—the Jews—and to a lesser extent, the Slavs. The program, which called for nothing less than the extermination of the Jewish people, came to be known, deceptively, as the "final solution." Hitler said he had "the right to eliminate millions of an inferior race that multiplies like vermin." Beginning in January, 1942, Jews from all over Europe were rounded up and shipped to concentration camps, most of them in eastern Germany and Poland. In the camps the SS developed techniques for mass slaughter in gas chambers by which as many as 25,000 Jews a day were put to death. Most notorious of all was Auschwitz, where more than a million men, women and children were murdered. When the whole horror was revealed after the war, it was calculated that nearly 6,000,000 persons had been killed.

Other atrocities were perpetrated in occupied lands, such as shooting ten hostages for one German killed by partisans. To keep up the production of war materials and to free German men for military service, the Germans brought in thousands of people from other lands, including Russian war prisoners, to work in factories and on farms. It is estimated that by September, 1944, 7,500,000 foreigners were working for the Germans as little better than slave laborers.

By 1945, Hitler was no longer in control of events and at times he admitted the war might be lost. If so, he said, it would be the fault of the German people who were proving not to be equal to his greatness. Yet Germany was sure to win, he said on another occasion, because it had to save Europe from Asia. He even asserted that he expected the western Allies to cease fighting him and join the Nazis in a war against Communist Russia. He did sense ahead of many others that Russia and the United States, if Germany lost, would emerge as the two great powers left in the world.

Hitler's health declined steadily after the first reverses on the Russian front. He had always been somewhat of a hypochondriac, suffering gastric pains and thinking his heart was bad or that he would die of cancer as his mother had. For many years he had been a vegetarian and as time went on subsisted more and more on such things as gruel, oatmeal soup and baked potatoes. He got almost no fresh air or exercise during the war, spending most of his time in bunkers at his various army headquarters. By 1945, although he was not yet fifty-six, he appeared to be on the verge of collapse. He was stooped and had a shuffling gait. His hands trembled and his left arm twitched violently. Hitler was also taking numerous drugs—sometimes as many as twenty-eight—prescribed by a doctor in whom he had great faith but who was either incompetent or a quack. Much of the time the Führer sat slumped in a daze but every so often roused himself and became enraged as he talked about those he thought had failed him.

On January 16, 1945, Hitler arrived in Berlin and went to live in the air raid bunker under the Chancellery, which itself was by now largely bombed out. Here he made sporadic attempts to command what was left of the German armed forces, which were being pushed back steadily by the Russians on the east and the Americans, British and Free French on the west. He alternated between denunciations of the generals and the nation and unrealistic orders for attacks by divisions that no longer existed. While his troops everywhere had no choice but to retreat or be killed, he still ordered them never to give ground. As Martin Bormann, Hitler's personal secretary, wrote his wife, life under the Chancellery reminded him of "those old boys in the Nibelungen in King Etzel's [Attila's] hall," before *Götterdämmerung*—the Twilight of the Gods.

Among the small group awaiting the now inevitable catastrophe was Eva Braun, whom Hitler had met in 1929 when she was a photographer's assistant. She had been his mistress for many years and came to Berlin of her own free will to be with him at the end. Around midnight on April 28—29, Adolf Hitler and Eva Braun were married in the bunker and a wedding party of sorts was contrived. The next day, April 30, with Russian artillery shells falling on the Chancellery, Eva took poison and Hitler shot himself in the head. Acting on his instructions, his aides took both bodies outside, poured gasoline on them and set them afire in the hope of preventing their identification by the victors. Hitler was joined in death by suicide by Goebbels, his wife and their six children. In a matter of days, the "thousand-year Reich" Hitler had proclaimed collapsed after a dozen years of bloodshed.

Adolf Hitler was perhaps the greatest demagogue in history. He was able, largely by the intensity of his drive to power, to seduce a civilized nation and its professional generals into performing cruel and irrational acts. His effectiveness as a speaker, with his highly emotional, hysterical performances that hypnotized audiences, and his astuteness as a politician are proved by his successes. He had one program: to achieve power for himself. And one plan: to expand German territory and prestige. He believed that history was made by great men and that destiny had selected him to be one of those great men. And history to him was all racial struggle and war. Many times he told listeners that everything depended on him, that he was irreplaceable and that he was born to be a dictator.

Hitler not only knew how to use propaganda effectively but he cynically, and often correctly, made the point that a big lie was the most effective kind. Although he set out to lead the masses, he had a low opinion of them. "The great masses of the people," he wrote, "will more easily fall victims to a big lie than to a small one." He had no scruples about lying, practicing treachery or using any other means to gain power. Brute force was to be applied as needed. "The one means that wins the easiest victory over reason," he wrote, is "terror and force." For a short time he was the most powerful and the most feared man on earth. And although the Nazi system disappeared when he died, he had in a dozen years changed the world so that it would never be the same again.

In spite of the terror that came to be associated with his name, Hitler was, at least for a while, an object of fun to outsiders. At first it was not easy to take seriously this strutting, nondescript man, with his toothbrush mustache and the lock of hair hanging down over his forehead. Charlie Chaplin satirized him in the movie "The Great Dictator" in 1940, including the mustache Chaplin had made famous many years earlier as the Tramp and which was much like Hitler's.

To the end, Hitler often acted like a frustrated architect. He had plans for the postwar era when he would build in Berlin a great domed hall, nearly 900 feet high, that would hold 180,000 people. Even when bombs were falling on Berlin, he spent hours admiring models of other buildings and monuments he would some day erect.

Something about destruction on a large scale fascinated Hitler. Toward the end, if there was to be a catastrophe, he wanted it to be the greatest catastrophe possible in order to bring everyone and everything down with him. At one point he issued orders, which fortunately were not obeyed, that as the German army withdrew into Germany it should destroy everything usable. He meant not just buildings and factories but food, appliances, even works of art. His twisted outlook on history and the human race is expressed in *Mein Kampf:* "Mankind has grown strong in eternal struggle and it will only perish through eternal peace."

# Are "Great Men" Great?

The eight men whose life stories have been told in this book were "great" in the sense that they had enormous, even shattering, effects on the people under them, their nations, their enemies, their times and, therefore, on the future of the world or part of it. They "made history." They were individuals who lived and acted out their careers in public while the great masses of the people remained unknown except to families and friends. They became historical figures whom the world must continue to take into account so long as history is recorded and studied in any attempt to understand the evolution of human society. The condition of the human race at any time depends in part on earlier events. Knowledge of the past may help chart and possibly guide the future, if mankind so wishes.

In their own day, all these men were great, at least in their own eyes, for practical reasons as well. They ruled over large numbers of people and determined how those people should live, how they should prosper or suffer. Most of them showed their power by leading armies to victory over outside enemies. In some cases they acquired great wealth for themselves and some of their subjects as a result of their conquests. The record of their lives and actions shows that they took much pleasure in holding the positions they did and performing the deeds they did.

It ought to be kept in mind that in spite of the suffering they brought to millions, there were just as many people who gladly followed them in their quests and obeyed them unquestioningly. A shortage of assistant tyrants and deputy conquerors never existed. Ironically, as the record shows, a good many of these high-ranking followers fell from favor and suffered the same fate as those they had previously helped rule and persecute. Even in the lower ranks, tyrants and conquerors were followed willingly by thousands and thousands for the sake of booty or for such abstract concepts as nation or race.

These eight and others like them have at least one thing in common—they wanted absolute power and they enjoyed exercising it, whether they inherited it or fought to acquire it. Nor did any of them have any scruples about how they exercised their power or what means they used to secure whatever ends they wanted to achieve. They showed a basic urge to get power—to be a successful tyrant—and to use that power as they pleased. They also share the burden of having caused the deaths, in total, of millions of people, most of them innocent of any wrongdoing against these rulers.

There are many differences, too. For example, only in the cases of Muhammad and Hitler were they much influenced by ideology, that is, the furtherance of a cause, rather than an urge for personal or dynastic power. Six of them were conquerors, but Nero and Ivan do not deserve that title as military commanders. Neither showed any desire to lead armies nor any ability on the battlefield. Of the six who were conquerors, five were extremely successful and died when their military gains were at their greatest. Hitler, however, ended by being crushingly defeated. All except Hitler inherited some measure, no matter how small, of rank or power. He alone rose from nothing. He also was the only one, among a group consisting of Shih Huang-ti, Attila, Jenghiz Khan and Tamerlane, who secured power, or greatly increased his power, other than by force of arms. Nero, Muhammad and Ivan started at the top.

Nero and Ivan were cowards, Hitler was a demagogue, the rest were essentially warriors. As to overall careers, Nero, Ivan and Hitler have to be judged failures, but the others were quite successful in terms of their own goals. Only Shih Huang-ti, Jenghiz Khan and Muhammad can be said to have done anything constructive and these accomplishments were largely offset by their destructive actions. In passing such judgments, the question always arises as to whether judgment should be made in relation to today's standards or the standards of the time and place in which the man lived. On the latter basis, Nero, Tamerlane and Hitler performed worse acts than were in accordance with the standards of their times. The others were about in accord with contemporary customs.

As human beings with individual personalities, they do not seem to have had many traits in common. Far and away the most degenerate in his personal life was Nero who, however, caused the fewest deaths. Hitler lived a quite austere personal life. Nero and Hitler committed suicide when their worlds collapsed around them. The others, even though most of them were in combat many times, died in bed. Ivan and Hitler were given to hysterical rages and Nero was extremely emotional. The rest, according to most accounts, seldom if ever lost control of their feelings and were known for their calmness in times of stress. Shih Huang-ti, Attila, Jenghis Khan and Muhammad have reputations as honorable men, so far as we can judge, men who kept their word and abided by whatever the rules of the time were. Nero, Tamerlane and Hitler can only be described as liars who practiced treachery as a way of life.

It is tempting to speculate as to what these men would have thought of each other, for despite their differences they have more in common with each other than with ordinary human beings. Would Muhammad understand why Hitler murdered the Jews of the Warsaw ghetto as he did; and would Hitler understand why Muhammad slaughtered the Christians of Smyrna as he did? Attila probably would wonder why Hitler didn't execute all the inhabitants of Paris when the German army captured it in 1940. Ivan with his Oprichniki would appreciate Hitler's Gestapo. Shih Huang-ti would have found nothing strange in the burning by the Nazis of books whose contents they did not like. Jenghiz Khan, especially, would have understood Hitler's drive for *Lebensraum* for his own people at the expense of whoever was in the way.

This they did have in common: not one of them exercised his power for the cultural and spiritual good of the individuals who were dependent on his rule. At best, they thought in terms of killing others for booty for their people, or of increasing the prestige and power of the nation or race.

Does history teach lessons? And if so, what lessons do the lives of these tyrants and conquerors teach? Lord Acton (1834–1902), the English historian who hated arbitrary power, concluded that "great men are almost always bad men." He also said: "Power tends to corrupt and absolute power corrupts absolutely."

Over the centuries, however, a great many people seem to have accepted such a state of affairs. One man's cruel tyrant has been another man's willingly accepted ruler; one man's bloodthirsty conqueror has been another man's deserving victor.

# For Further Reading

## General

HARRIS, WILLIAM H., and LEVEY, JUDITH S. (eds.). *The New Columbia Encyclopedia*. New York: Columbia University Press, 1975.

McNEILL, WILLIAM H. *The Rise of the West; A History of the Human Community*. Chicago, Ill.: University of Chicago Press, 1963.

———. *A World History*. 2nd ed. New York: Oxford University Press, 1971.

TOYNBEE, ARNOLD. *A Study of History*. A New Edition, Revised and Abridged. New York: Oxford University Press, 1972.

## Shih Huang-ti

BODDE, DERK. *China's First Unifier; A Study of the Ch'in Dynasty as Seen in the Life of Li Ssu*. Hong Kong: Hong Kong University Press, 1967.

COTTERELL, LEONARD. *The Tiger of Ch'in; The Dramatic Emergence of China as a Nation*. New York: Holt, Rinehart and Winston, 1962.

GOODRICH, L. CARRINGTON. *A Short History of the Chinese People*. 3rd ed. New York: Harper & Row, 1959.

GROUSSET, RENÉ. *The Rise and Splendour of the Chinese Empire*. Berkeley, Calif.: University of California Press, 1968.

HOOKHAM, HILDA. *A Short History of China.* New York: New American Library, 1972.

HUCKER, CHARLES O. *China's Imperial Past; An Introduction to Chinese History and Culture.* Stanford, Calif.: Stanford University Press, 1975.

LI, DUN J. *The Ageless Chinese; A History.* 2nd ed. New York: Charles Scribner's Sons, 1971

## Nero

BISHOP, JOHN. *Nero; The Man and the Legend.* New York: A. S. Barnes & Co., 1964.

DIO CASSIUS. *Roman History.* Vol. VIII. Cambridge, Mass.: Harvard University Press, 1925.

GRANT, MICHAEL. *Nero; Emperor in Revolt.* New York: American Heritage Press, 1970.

HAMMOND, N. G., and SCULLARD, H. H. (eds.). *The Oxford Classical Dictionary.* 2nd ed. New York: Oxford University Press, 1970.

SUETONIUS TRANQUILLUS, GAIUS. *The Twelve Caesars.* Baltimore, Md.: Penguin Books, 1957.

TACITUS. *The Annals of Imperial Rome.* Baltimore, Md.: Penguin Books, 1959.

WARMINGTON, B. H. *Nero: Reality and Legend.* New York: W. W. Norton & Co., Inc., 1969.

## Attila

COSTAIN, THOMAS B. *The Darkness and the Dawn: A Novel.* Garden City, N.Y.: Doubleday & Co., 1959.

GORDON, C. D. *The Age of Attila; Fifth-Century Byzantium and the Barbarians.* Ann Arbor, Mich.: University of Michigan Press, 1960.

GROUSSET, RENÉ. *The Empire of the Steppes; A History of Central Asia.* New Brunswick, N.J.: Rutgers University Press, 1970.

MAENCHEN-HELFEN, OTTO J. *The World of the Huns; Studies in Their History and Culture.* Berkeley, Calif.: University of California Press, 1973.

THOMPSON, E. A. *A History of Attila and the Huns.* New York: Oxford University Press, 1948. (Reprinted 1975 by Greenwood Press.)

## Jenghiz Khan.

BLUNT, WILFRID. *The Golden Road to Samarkand.* New York: The Viking Press, 1973.

GROUSSET, RENÉ. *Conqueror of the World; The Life of Chingis-Khan.* New York: The Viking Press, 1972.

LISTER, R. P. *Genghis Khan.* New York: Stein & Day, 1969.

PRAWDIN, MICHAEL. *The Mongol Empire: Its Rise and Legacy.* New York: The Free Press, 1967. (First published 1940.)

VLADIMIRTSOV, BORIS. *The Life of Chingis-Khan.* New York: Benjamin Blom, 1969. (First published 1930.)

See also the book by Grousset listed under Attila.

## Tamerlane

HOOKHAM, HILDA. *Tamburlaine the Conqueror.* London: Hodder & Stoughton, 1962.

See also the book by Grousset listed under Attila and the books by Blunt and Prawdin listed under Jenghiz Khan.

## Muhammad II

DAVISON, RODERIC H. *Turkey.* Englewood Cliffs, N.J.: Prentice-Hall, Inc., 1968.

GUERDAN, RENÉ. *Byzantium: Its Triumphs and Tragedy.* New York: Capricorn Books, 1962.

KINROSS, LORD. *The Ottoman Centuries; The Rise and Fall of the Turkish Empire.* New York: William Morrow & Co., 1977.

KRITOVOULOS. *History of Mehmed the Conqueror.* Princeton, N.J.: Princeton University Press, 1954. (Reprinted 1970 by Greenwood Press.)

RUNCIMAN, STEVEN. *The Fall of Constantinople, 1453.* New York: Cambridge University Press, 1965.

SHAW, STANFORD. *History of the Ottoman Empire and Modern Turkey. Vol. I: Empire of the Gazis: The Rise and Decline of the Ottoman Empire, 1280–1808.* New York: Cambridge University Press, 1976.

VUCINICH, WAYNE S. *The Ottoman Empire; Its Record and Legacy.* Princeton, N.J.: D. Van Nostrand Co., 1965.

## Ivan the Terrible

GRAHAM, STEPHEN. *Ivan the Terrible; Life of Ivan IV of Russia.* London: Ernest Benn, 1933. (Reprinted 1968 by Archon Books.)

KOSLOW, JULES. *Ivan the Terrible.* New York: Hill & Wang, 1961.

PAYNE, ROBERT, and ROMANOFF, NIKITA. *Ivan the Terrible.* New York: Thomas Y. Crowell Co., 1975.

PIPES, RICHARD. *Russia Under the Old Regime.* New York: Charles Scribner's Sons, 1974.

RIASANOVSKY, NICHOLAS V. *A History of Russia.* New York: Oxford University Press, 1963.

## Adolf Hitler

BULLOCK, ALAN. *Hitler; A Study in Tyranny.* Rev. ed. New York: Harper & Row, 1962.

FEST, JOACHIM C. *Hitler.* New York: Harcourt Brace Jovanovich, 1973.

HITLER, ADOLF. *Mein Kampf.* Boston, Mass.: Houghton Mifflin Co., 1943.

MASER, WERNER. *Hitler; Legend, Myth and Reality.* New York: Harper & Row, 1973.

SHIRER, WILLIAM L. *The Rise and Fall of the Third Reich; A History of Nazi Germany.* New York: Simon & Schuster, 1959.

TOLAND, JOHN. *Adolf Hitler.* Garden City, N.Y.: Doubleday & Co., 1976.

# Index

Acte, 36, 44
Acton, Lord, 172
Adashev, Alexei, 130, 131, 137, 138
Aetius, 58, 63, 64
Afghanistan, 80, 82, 83
agriculture, 17, 48, 51, 79-80, 87
Agrippina, 27-29, 35-36, 37
Ahenobarbus, Gnaeus Domitius, 27
Ahmed Jelair, 98
Alans, 63
Alaric I, 4, 55
Albania, 116, 118
Alexander the Great, 4, 13, 81, 96
Ali-Bek, 91
Alshai, 90, 91
Amin, Idi, 3
Amiroukis, George, 117
Ammianus Marcellinus, 53
Anatolia. See Asia Minor
Anicetus, 36
Anti-Comintern Pact, 158
anti-Semitism, 146, 148, 150-51, 152, 156, 159, 164
Arcadius, 55
architecture, 17-18, 19, 22, 40-41, 87, 100, 101, 112, 113, 144, 167
Armenia, 34, 56, 98
Arnegisclus, 60
art, 38-39, 41, 65, 100, 101, 113, 121
Asia Minor, 32, 98, 104, 106, 108, 117, 118, 119
Astrakhan Khanate, 132-33
Athanaric, 54-55
Attila, 6, 47-48, 51, 56-66, 102, 166, 170-71

Augustus, 27, 28, 30, 32
Auschwitz, 164
Austria, 143, 150, 154, 158
Austro-Hungarian Empire, 143, 144
Avars, 55

Babur, 4
Balkans, 98, 108, 115, 116, 119, 161
barbarians, 20, 50
Barlas, Hazii, 90-91
Barlas tribe, 87, 91
Battle of the Bulge, 164
Batu Khan, 84
Bayezit (son of Muhammad II), 120-21
Bayezit I, 98
Beer Hall Putsch. See Munich Putsch
Belgium, 146, 149, 160, 164
Bellini, Gentile, 121
Berlin, 149, 163, 165
Bible, The, 44-45
Bleda, 57, 58
Blitzkrieg, 159
Boadicea. See Boudicca
Bokassa, Jean Bedel, 3
Bolívar, Simón, 2-3
books, burning of, 20-21, 155, 172
Bo'orchu, 70
Borman, Martin, 166
Borte, 70, 72, 74
Boudicca, 3-4, 34
boyars, 126-29, 131-32, 139, 140, 142
Braun, Eva, 166
Britannicus, 28, 30, 35, 36

Bulgaria, 118, 161, 164
Burgundians, 58
Burrus, 31, 32-33, 35, 37, 42
Bursah Ahmet Pasa, 115
Byzantine Empire. See East
   Roman Empire

Caligula, 27
Calixtus II, Pope, 103
Calpurnius, 38
Carpini, Giovanni, 68
Catherine the Great, 3
Cem Sultan, 119, 120
Chamberlain, Neville, 158
Chancellor, Richard, 131, 141
Ch'ang Ch'un, 82-83
Chao Kao, 22-24
Chaplin, Charlie, 167
Charlemagne, 4
Cheliadnin, Ivan, 140
Chen Seng, 23
Cheng, King. See Shi Huang-ti
Ch'in Dynasty, 7, 12-25
China, 7-25, 73-74, 78, 79, 82, 83,
   84, 100
Chou Dynasty, 8-10, 14
Christians and Christianity, 41, 45,
   52, 66, 81-82, 99, 101-2, 108,
   109, 112, 113, 124, 126, 151,
   171
Chrysaphius, 60
Claudius, 27-30, 31
commerce, 80, 96, 99-100, 113,
   115, 131, 134, 141
Communism and Communists,
   148, 151, 152, 155, 158, 159,
   165
Comnenus, David, 117
Comnenus family, 117
Concentration camps, 156, 159,
   164
Confucianism, 12, 15, 24
Confucius, 10, 12
conquerors, 2-4, 169-72
conquistadores, 2
Constantine XI, 108, 109, 110, 112,
   124
Constantinople, 55, 59, 60-61, 98,
   106, 108-14

Corbulo, 34, 43
Corinth Canal, 42
cowards, 170
Crimea, the, 119-20, 135-36
Crimean Khanate, 135-36, 140
Crispinus, Rufius, 40
crusades, 81, 106, 108, 117, 118,
   120
currency, 17, 31
Cyrus the Great, 4
Czechoslovakia, 154, 158, 159

d'Aubusson, Pierre, 120
David, King, 82
Dawes Plan, 146
Delhi Sultanate, 96-97
Denmark, 160, 162
Depression, the, 152
Dio Cassius, 30-31, 34, 39, 44
Dmitri (son of Ivan the Terrible),
   129, 131-32
Dmitri Donskoi, 124
Domus Aurea, 40-41
Druids, 33
Duvalier, François, 2, 3

East Roman Empire, 47, 51, 55-56,
   57, 58, 59-60, 64, 99, 104, 106,
   108, 113, 117, 124, 128
Eastern Orthodox Church, 113,
   124, 134
Edeco, 60-61
Egypt, 32, 81, 97
Elizabeth, Queen, 141
Ellac, 65
England, 32, 33-34, 131, 141, 142
Erh-shih Huang-ti, 23-24
Ermanaric, 54
Ertugrul, 104
Etzel, 66, 166
Eudocia, 56, 59

Feodor, Tsar, 141-42
feudalism, 8, 16, 24
food, 33, 40, 48, 51, 61, 90
France, 146, 149, 157, 158-59, 160
Franco, Francisco, 157
Fu-su, 21, 22-23

Gainas, 57
Gaiseric, 4
Galba, 43, 44
Gandhi, Indira, 3
Gaul, 43, 63
Genoa, 110, 118, 119
Georgia, 99
Gepids, 60, 65
Germanicus, 27
Germany, 130, 134, 143-67
Gestapo, 157, 171
Giorgi VI, 99
Giustiniani, Giovanni, 110, 112
Glinsky, Helena, 123, 126
Glinsky, Prince Michael, 126
Godunov, Boris, 142
Goebbels, Paul Joseph, 152, 155, 166
Goering, Hermann, 149, 156, 157
Golden Horde, 94-95, 96, 119, 124, 132, 135
Goths, 54-55, 57, 60, 63
government, systems of, 10-12, 15-17, 32, 51-52, 77, 90, 114, 130, 138, 154, 155, 167, 170
Grand Duchy of Moscow, 123-24
Great Britain, 157, 158, 159, 160, 162. *See also* England
great men, 169-72
Great Wall of China, 19-20, 50, 78
Greece, 31, 38, 41-42, 106, 116, 118, 161
Gundahar, 58

Hafiz, 94
Halil, 114
Han Dynasty, 8, 24
Han Fei, 15-16
Hastings, Lady Mary, 141
Herculanus, 62
Hereca, 62
Hess, Rudolph, 150
Himmler, Heinrich, 156-57
Hindenburg, Paul von, 149, 153, 154, 155, 157
historians, 4, 7-8, 10, 13, 14, 18, 22, 30-31, 53-54, 68, 88, 97, 102, 106
Hitler, Adolph, 3, 143-67, 170-72

Hoelun, 67, 70, 78
Honoria, 62
Honorius, 55
horses, 13, 39, 52-53, 68, 70, 76, 78, 79, 85, 96
Hsia Dynasty, 8
Hsi-Hsia, 78, 83
Hsiung-nu, 20, 50
Hu-hai. *See* Erh-shih Huang-ti
Huma Hatum, 103
Hungary, 106, 161
Huns, 4, 20, 47-66, 67, 76, 104
hunting, 51, 68, 83, 85, 90
Hunyadi, John, 106, 116
Husain, 90, 91-92
Husain Sufi, 93
Hyacinth, 62

Ibn Arabshah, Ahmad, 88, 97
Ibn Khaldun, 97
Iceni, 33-34
Ildico, 64-65
Ili, 90, 91-92, 93
Ilyas-khoja, 91
India, 80, 96-97
Iraq, 98
Islam, 80, 87, 96, 97, 100, 101, 103, 104, 109, 112, 113
Italy, 64, 120, 158
Ivan (the tsarevitch), 133, 135, 141
Ivan III, 124
Ivan (IV) the Terrible, 2, 3, 123-42, 170-71

Jagatai, 72, 84, 87
Jagatai Khanate, 92
Jahangir, 93
Jamuqa, 72-73, 76
Janissary Corps, 114-15, 120
Japan, 158, 162
Jebe, 75, 80
Jelal ud-Din, 82
Jelmei, 75
Jenghiz Khan, 4, 6, 50, 67-85, 87, 88, 90, 92, 93, 99, 102, 124, 170-72
Jews, 34-35, 146, 148, 150-51, 152, 156, 159, 164, 171
Jochi, 72, 84, 93-94

Jordanes, 53-54, 63
Judaea, 34-35
Juvaini, 68

Kara-Khitai, 80, 84
Karamania, 118-19
Kazan Khanate, 131
Keraits, 72, 76
Khalil, 101
Khwarazm Empire, 81-82, 84, 87, 91, 93
Kipchak Khanate. See Golden Horde
Knights Hospitalers, 99, 120-21
Kokchu, 78
Kremlin, 126, 128, 129, 131, 135
Kritovoulos, 106, 116, 117, 121
Kublai, Khan, 83, 84
Kuchlug, 80
Kurbsky, Prince Andrei, 132, 138
Kuzgan, Emir, 90

Ladislaus III, 106
language, 4, 20, 77
Lao-tze, 10
League of Nations, 146, 151, 156
Lebensraum, 151, 161, 172
legal systems, 13-14, 17, 77, 90, 113-14, 130
Legalism, 15, 17, 23, 24
Leo I, Pope, 64
Li An-ch'uan, 78
Li Ssu, 16, 19, 20-21, 22-23
literature, 20-21, 38, 66, 101, 102, 115, 121
Lithuania, 133-34, 136, 138
Liu Pang, 24
Livonia, 133-34, 136, 138, 141
Locusta, 28, 36
Lucan, 38
Ludendorff, Erich, 149
Luftwaffe, 160
Lu Pu-wei, 7
Luxembourg, 160

McNeill, William H., 102
Maginot Line, 159
Mahmud II, 96-97

Mamelukes, 97, 98
Mansur, Shah, 94
Mara, 194
Marcian, 56, 61, 62, 64
Marlowe, Christopher, 102
Marxism and Marxists. See Communism
Mary I, Queen, 142
Maximinus, 60-61
Mein Kampf, 150, 167
Mencius, 10, 12
Meng T'ien, 20, 21, 22-23
Merkits, 72, 73, 74
Messalina, Statilis, 37-38
Messalina, Valeria, 28
Middle Ages, 113
Ming Dynasty, 100
Miran Shah, Prince, 95, 99
Mogholistan, 93
Moldavia, 119
Mongolia, 67-68, 74, 75, 76, 78, 84, 105
Mongols, 4, 48, 50, 67-85, 87, 92, 95, 99, 101, 104, 119, 124
Moscow, 124-26, 129-30, 133, 135, 140, 161
Moslems, 87, 90, 104
Muhammad II, 4, 6, 103-22, 170-71
Muhammad, Shah, 80-81
Muhammad, Sultan, 100
Mundich, 57
Munich, 144, 148, 149
Munich Pact, 158-59
Munich Putsch, 149
Muquli, 79
Murad I, 114
Murad II, 103, 106, 116
Mussolini, Benito, 158, 161, 163

Naimans, 73, 75, 76, 77, 80
Napoleon Bonaparte, 4
National Socialist German Workers' Party. See Nazi Party
Nazi Party, 148-49, 151-52, 153-54, 155, 158
Nero, 27-45, 170-71
Netherlands, The, 160

Ngueno, Macias, 3
Nibelungen, 66
nomads, 20, 48-53, 84
Normandy, 163
North Africa, 32, 161, 162
Norway, 160
Novgorod, 124, 134-35, 136
Nuremberg, 152
Nuremberg Laws, 159

Oblensky, Prince, 126-28
Octar, 57
Octavia, 28, 36-37
Ogodai, 72, 84
Onegesius, 61
Oprichniki, 139-40, 171
Oprichnina, 139-40
Osman I, 104
Ostrogoths, 54, 65
Otho, 37
Ottoman Turks, 98-99, 103-22, 135

Papen, Franz von, 153-54
Parthian Empire, 34, 44
Pascal II, Pope, 45
Pearl Harbor, 162
Peking, 73, 79, 83
Persia, 80, 82, 84, 93-94, 95
Petronius, 38
Philip II, 13
Philip, Metropolitan, 139-40
Pir Ahmet, 118
Pir Muhammad, 96, 101
Pirenne, Henri, 102
Piso, 42-43
Pius II, Pope, 118
Placidia, 62
Plautus, Rubellius, 40
Polo, Marco, 68
Poland, 106, 133, 136, 151, 159, 163, 164
Poppaea, 36-37, 38
Praetorian Guard, 30, 31-32, 38, 43, 114
Prester John, 82
Priscus, 47, 53, 61-62
Ptolemy, 117
Pulcheria, 56

Qamar ad-Din, 93
Qasar, 78
Qulan, 74-75

Reichstag, 152, 153, 155
religion, 41, 45, 52, 77-78, 80, 87, 90, 96, 97, 101, 126, 142
Renaissance, 113
reparations, 146, 149, 152
Rhineland, 146, 157
Roehm, Ernst, 152, 156
Roman Empire, 24, 27-45, 47, 50, 51, 54, 55, 65, 67, 108, 128
Romanov, Anastasia, 129, 137
Rome, 32, 40-41, 43, 113
Rome-Berlin Axis, 158
Rua, 57, 83
Ruhr, 149
Rukh, Shan, 94, 101
Rumania, 57, 117, 119, 161, 164
Runciman, Steven, 4-6, 121
Russia, 50, 83, 84, 94-95, 99, 113, 119, 123-42, 151, 159, 161-63, 164, 165

Sain Bulat, 140-41
St. Bartholomew's Day Massacre, 142
St. Jerome, 56
St. Paul, 41
St. Peter, 41
Samarkand, 80, 81, 83, 87, 88, 99-101
Saray-Mulk-Khanum, 92
Scanderberg, 116
Schicklgruber, Alois, 143
Schleicher, Kurt von, 154, 156
Schuschnigg, Kurt von, 158
*Schutzstaffel* (SS), 156-57, 164
science, 101, 115, 117, 121, 130
Scythians, 48, 50
Seljuk Turks, 80, 104
Senate, Roman, 28, 30, 31, 32
Seneca, 31, 32-33, 35, 37, 38, 42-43
Serbia, 116
Seyss-Inquart, Arthur, 158
Shakhovskoy, Prince Ivan, 134
Shang Yang, 13-14

Shang Dynasty, 8
Sharaf ad-Din, Ali, 88
Shigiktuku, 77, 82
Shih Huang-ti, 4, 7, 14-25, 170-71
Shuisky, Andrei, 128
Sidonius Apollinaris, 53
Sigismund II, 133
Sitt Hatun, 103
slavery, 31, 52, 96, 101, 124, 135,
    164
Slavs, 55, 150, 151, 164
Socialism, 148, 152, 156
"Son of Heaven," 10
Spain, 157
Ssu-ma Ch'ien, 7-8, 10, 13, 14, 18,
    22
Stalin, Joseph, 3, 4, 159
Stalingrad, 162
Staritsky, Prince Vladimir, 132
Stephen the Great, 119
steppes, 20, 48, 50-51, 67, 70, 84,
    88, 90, 194
Storm Troops (SA), 149, 152, 153,
    154, 156
Strasser, Gregor, 156
Sturmabteilung. See Storm Troops
Sudetenland, 158
Suetonius, 30-31, 40, 41
Suetonius Paulinus, 33
suicide, 38, 40, 43, 44, 166, 171
Suleiman the Magnificent, 121
Sweden, 133-34, 160
Sylvester, 130, 131, 137
Syria, 35

Tacitus, 30, 34, 37, 41
Taijuts, 70, 75
Tamerlane, 84, 87-102, 106, 119,
    170-71
Tanguts, 78
Taoism, 10, 15, 82
Tatars, 13, 67, 70, 74, 119, 124,
    126, 132
Tatatunga, 77
technology, 8, 19, 65, 109, 130
Temujin. See Jenghiz Khan
Teragai, 87
Teutons, 55

Theodoric, 63
Theodosius the Great, 55
Theodosius II, 56, 59, 61
Thrace, 57, 60, 103
Thrasea Paetus, 40
Tigellinus, 38
Tiridates, 34
Togrul, 72, 73-74, 75, 76
Togrul Bey, 104
Tolui, 72, 84
Toqtamish, 95-96
Toynbee, Arnold, 102
Transoxiana, 87, 90-93, 95
Treaty of Versailles, 146, 154, 157
Trebizond, 117, 118
Tughlugh Timur, 90-91
Turkestan, 80
Turks (Turkic), 48, 74, 76, 80, 87,
    93, 98-99, 101, 103-22
tyrants, 1-4, 169-72
Tz'u Hsi, 3

Uigurs, 77
Uldis, 57
United States, 162, 165
Urban, 109, 110
Uzun Hasan, 119

Valentinian III, 56, 62, 63
Vasilly, III, 123
Venice, 110, 116, 118, 119, 120
Vespasian, 35
Vienna, 143-44
Vincianus, Annius, 43
Vindex, Gaius Julius, 43
Visigoths, 54, 63
Viskovaty, Prince Ivan, 140
Vithimiris, 54
Vlad the Impaler, Prince, 117-18
Vologeses I, 34

Wagner, Richard, 66
Wallachia, 117, 118, 119
warfare, 12-14, 16-17, 24, 25, 33-
    35, 52-56, 58-60, 72-77, 78-83,
    88-99, 104-6, 109-12, 115-20,
    132-37, 144-46, 159-66, 170

Warring States era, 12-14
Washington, George, 2-3
West Roman Empire, 55, 56, 57, 58, 62, 63, 64
White Horde, 95
White Sheep Turkomans, 119
Wilhelm II, Kaiser, 146
women, 52, 61, 62, 68, 72, 85, 90, 124
World War I, 144-46, 151, 152
World War II, 159-66

Ye-lu Ch'u-ts'ai, 79, 81
Yesugei, 67, 70
Yisugen, 74
Yisui, 74
Young Plan, 152
Yugoslavia, 161
Yusuf Sufi, 93

Zaganos Pasa, 114
Zemshchina, 139, 140
Zerco, 57